GEOTECHNICAL ENGINEERING

TESTING MANUALS

**PART I
GEOTECHNICAL TESTING
LABORATORY MANUAL**

**PART II
GEOTECHNICAL - GEOHYDROLOGICAL
FIELD MANUAL**

HAMED S. SAEEDY

M. Sc. Ph.D. C. Eng. MICE, MASCE.
Professor & Consulting Engineer

To order additional copies of this book, contact:
Xlibris
1-888-795-4274
www.Xlibris.com
Orders@Xlibris.com
746537

BRIEF RESUME OF THE AUTHOR

Prof. Saeedy, completed his first engineering qualification (civil) at Kingston College, Surrey, England in 1962.

In the year 1969 he became the Chief Structural Engineer with Ardaman and Associate, Orlando, Florida.

He graduated from the Colorado State University with M.Sc. in 1968, in Structural Engineering.

Got his Ph.D. from Oklahoma State University, U.S.A. in Geotechnical Engineering In 1971. During that time he was teaching and granted research and teaching assistance for two years at the same university.

1971 through 1983 he was an associate professor, chairman of Civil Engineering Dept., and then became the Dean of the College of Engineering, University of Basra.

1981-1983, he was a visiting Professor at Sheffield University, UK.

1984-1990 he was a senior Researcher at Kuwait Institute for Scientific Research. Since 1971, he practiced Civil Engineering Consultancy on various local and regional civil and geotechnical engineering projects and challenging engineering problems.

He is a member of the Institutions for Civil Engineers and Chartered Engineers (London) since 1973, also a member of the American Society of Civil Engineers (New York).

Prof. Saeedy has published many scientific papers, consultancy legal reports, textbooks, and technical manuals.

Also has travelled worldwide, attending scientific conferences and seminars in his field of specialty. Pro. Saeedy as an International Engineering Consultant; owned and associates with various engineering consultancy bureaus, in the region and abroad.

PRESENTATION

To my family for their continuous patience and encouragement.

ACKNOWLEDGMENT

The author wishes to acknowledge and express his gratefulness and appreciation for their valuable assistance in the first edition, which was provided by his assisting engineers Mr. Alla Mulla senior geotechnical engineer, Mr. Waleed Abdulah and Miss. Gayda Al-Naimi, for their remarkable efforts in sighting the required references, codes of practice and standards during the preparation of the first draft this book. Thanks and appreciation extended to Kuwait Institute for Scientific Research for their help and encouragement while preparing the initial draft of the first edition.

Further gratitude are also expressed to Mrs. Nada Farhat and Mr. Bilal Assaad of Beirut, Lebanon, for their kind assistance in typing Part IV of the first edition.

PREFACE TO SECOND EDITION

This edition of the book has been updated and developed to provide more up to date information which is found of great use and value to practicing geotechnical engineers whether in office, laboratory or on site. In the process, some of the materials was omitted, where further addition was made to bring the book to be more useful, by including some new materials. The general theme of the book have been changed to an eBook to be commensurate with latest digital development. The part of the technical expression in other language has been deleted since currently dictionary has been made available in all smart phones.

PART I
Contents

List of Tables

List of Figures

PART II
Contents

List of Tables

List of Figures

PART I

GEOTECHNICAL TESTING
LABORATORY MANUAL

PREFACE

Soil is defined as an uncemented naturally occuring material formed by a heterogynous accumulation of mineral particles. The particles vary in sizes, shapes and structures and they occur in various proportions as well as degrees of packing. Moreover, the mass may contain air, water or organic matter in varying proportions. All these factors act together to make phenomenon of soil behaviour complex and often unpredictable to give rise to problems like bearing capacity and settlement of structures, stability of slopes, pore water pressure, dewatering, earthwork, earth pressure, flow of water in soils, soil improvement etc. Professionals in the field of geotechnical engineering combat these problems by conducting a soil investigation. A laboratory investigation in complementary to field investigation serves two fold objectives:

1) Identification and classification into groups having identical engineering properties so as to make it possible to exchange information,

2) Facilitate counteracting of the soil problems effectively by evaluating the performance characteristics of soil. Soils as an engineering material found by natural processes but utilized by engineers to provide the adequate support as a foundation material or it is to be dealt with for stability purposes whether during short or long term behaviour. It is therefore very essential for soil to be subjected to a variety of testing and that needs to be programmed according to categories permitting to its type and condition.

1. INTRODUCTION

The primary intention to prepare this manual is to apprise the field staff to be engaged on this job on the objective of laboratory soil testing required, with the Soil Investigation Work for Civil Engineering, or building purposes, and then to train them on practical soil testing in the laboratory.

As a natural material, soil is found to form the following types:

o   Cohesive soils:
This includes soft, stiff and varved clay. This type of soil is known for its internal cohesion as a measure of its shear strength, mostly they are the least permeable.

o   Non-cohesive soils:
They are recognized by their internal friction resistance, this is produced as a result of the granular interlocking as the case in the fine, medium and coarse sands, and they exhibit the highest permeability as a soil media, it may be in a loose or densified state.

o   Silt soils:
This is other the last major group of soil which exhibits the two extreme properties of both clay and sand combined together from all aspects, shear strength, compressibility, water conveyance and all other common properties.

The soil tests which have been discovered throughout the recent decades are to pin point the marginal limits of each soil type, this of course would enable the professionals to apply the appropriate rules of mechanics accordingly in their term of design analysis involvements.

The most difficult part of laboratory investigation is the formulation of the testing program which requires to define clearly the purpose of each test to the programmer himself and others involved in it, and the type of soil to be tested. The testing manual, however, deals with the laboratory soil testing program within the scope of the required Geotechnical studies.

Some laboratory testing procedures are, nowadays, well documented in Standards like American Society for Testing Materials (ASTM), British Standards, (BS) etc. while others require modification one way or another. In this manual it is attempted to summarize, whenever necessary, the recommended testing procedures and to present them with considerable input from the experience with local soils in order to accommodate the specific requirements of this project.

While laying down procedures of the tests, attempts were made to group them, primarily based on their application to the appropriate engineering problems as follows:

- Soil Classification tests
- Soil Strength tests
- Soil Compressibility tests
- Soil Permeability tests
- Soil Chemical tests

2. SOIL CLASSIFICATION TESTS

Basically these test programs comprised of all the routine tests necessary for the determination of the physical and basic properties of soil. These tests mainly aim at describing and classifying soil into categories so as to be able to assess logical values for certain engineering properties where detailed data is not available. Two principal classification methods like Unified Soil Classification System (USCS) and U.S. Public Road classification make use of the analyses of data from these tests. To arrive at a general consensus about testing procedures, leading Standards like ASTM, BS, DIN etc. have standardized the method of determination.

Among these categories, the moisture content tests are devised to provide the required information, particularly the limiting values of moisture content are used to identify the well known (Atterberg limits). This is specially used in connection with cohesive soils.

2.1 DETERMINATION OF MOISTURE CONTENT OF SOIL SAMPLE

Scope:

This test covers the determination of the moisture content of soil as a percentage of its dry mass. Determination of moisture content is a routine test with soil laboratory investigation. The water held within the pore spaces of soil grains are removed by oven drying. ASTM D2216 specifies an oven temperature of $110\pm 5°C$.

This test is particularly important for fine grained soils which exhibit transitional limits of physical characteristics with moisture content.

Apparatus:.

○ Drying oven

Thermostatical control and

Capable of maintaining a temperature of 105° to 110°C

○ Balances: Precision

For mass of specimen 200 gm or less ± 0.01 gm For mass of specimen 200-1000 gm ± 0.1 gm For mass of specimen over 1000 gm ± 1.0 gm

○ Containers

Non-corroded

Close fitting lids for specimen mass of 200 gm or less

○ Desiccator containing silica gel.

Recommended only when containers with close fitting lids are not used.

Preparation of Test Sample:

○ Mix the sample thoroughly. Divide the sample by riffling (Fig. 1), from ASTM, 1982, Part 14, p.458, or by quartering technique (Fig. 2).

Take Mass of moist material as follows:

fine grained soil	30 gm
medium grained soil	300 gm
coarse grained soil	3000 gm

Test Procedure:

○ Select and place the moist specimen in a clean, dry container of known mass. Replace the lid and weigh the container with its contents.

Figure 1. Riffle Box

Cone sample   Quartering sample

Retain opposite quaters

Figure 2. Quartering on a Hard Clean Level Surface

SOIL MECHANICS LABORATORY

DETERMINATION OF MOISTURE CONTENT AND VOID RATIO OF SOIL

JOB NO.	TEST DATE
LOCATION	PROJECT
BORING NO.	SAMPLE DESCRIPTION:
SAMPLE NO.	SPECIFIC GRAVITY OF SOIL, G_s:
SAMPLE DEPTH, m	TESTED BY:	SUPERVISOR:

A. DETERMINATION OF MOISTURE CONTENT OF SOIL

CONDITION	TARE NO.	WEIGHT IN GM OF			MOISTURE CONTENT, (%)
		TARE	TARE + MOIST SOIL	TARE + DRY SOIL	
		m_1	m_2	m_3	w
INITIAL					
FINAL					

B. DETERMINATION OF UNIT WEIGHT & VOID RATIO OF SOIL

CONDITION	SAMPLE TUBE			WEIGHT IN GM OF			BULK UNIT WEIGHT, kg/m^3	DRY UNIT WEIGHT, kg/m^3	VOID RATIO
	DIAMETER, cm	HEIGHT, cm	VOLUME, cc	TUBE + MOIST SOIL	TUBE	MOIST SOIL			
	D	H	V			W	γ_b	γ_d	e
INITIAL									
FINAL									

FORMULAE:

1. $w = \dfrac{m_2 - m_3}{m_3 - m_1} \times 100$ (%)

2. $\gamma_b = \dfrac{W}{V} \times 1000$ (kg/m^3)

3. $\gamma_d = \dfrac{\gamma_b}{1 + w/100}$ (kg/m^3)

4. $e = \dfrac{G.\gamma_w}{\gamma_d} - 1$

REMARKS:

_____
_____
_____
_____
_____

- ○ Remove the lid to place underneath and then place the container with moist material in the oven maintaining at 105°C to 110°C and leave it at least for 16 hours.
- ○ After drying the specimen replace the lid and allow the sample to cool down.
- ○ Weigh the container and contents.

Calculation:.

Calculate the moisture content as follows:

$$w\,(\%) = \frac{m_2 - m_3}{m_3 - m_1} \times 100 \tag{1}$$

where

m_1 = mass of container, gm
m_2 = mass of container and moist soil, gm
m_3 = mass of container and dry soil, gm

Reporting:

Report w (%) to two significant figures.

2.2   DETERMINATION OF LIQUID LIMIT OF SOILS

Liquid Limit (w_L) and Plastic Limit (w_p), well-known as Atterberg Limits in Soil Mechanics are two of the five limits for w_p cohesive soil were first proposed by A. Atterberg, a Swedish Agricultural Scientist, (Ca. 1911). However, a definite definition of Liquid Limit was proposed by A. Casagrande (Ca. 1932). Plasticity Index (I_p) of soil, measured as follows:

$$I_p\,(\%) = w_L - w_p$$
$$\text{where } w_L = \text{Liquid Limit (\%)}$$
$$w_p = \text{Plastic Limit (\%)} \qquad \cdot \tag{2}$$

is an indication of the plasticity of the soil.
The relative locations of wL, wp and Ip on the
moisture contents scale are shown in Fig. 3.

Although empirical, the Atterberg Limits determination provide a good indication of many engineering properties particularly pertaining to cohesive soils. The Liquid Limit and Plasticity Index are mainly used for classification of fine grained soil. Engineering properties of different types of soil are given in Table 1.

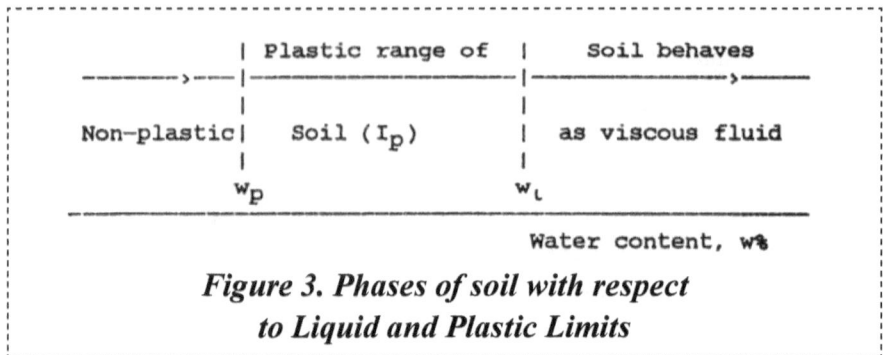

Figure 3. Phases of soil with respect to Liquid and Plastic Limits

Scope:

This test covers the determination of the Liquid Limit of the air dried soil using a Casagrande apparatus.

○ Evaporation dish or flat glass plate (500 mm square)

Table 1. Engineering Properties of Different types of soil (Saeedy, 1980)

(USES OF CLAYEY SOIL ACCORDING TO DEGREE OF PLASTICITY)

Plasticity Index, I_p (%)	Degree of Plasticity	Type of Soil	Engineering Properties
0-1	Non-Plastic	Silt	Crushable
1-5	Little Plasticity	Partially Clayey	Likely acceptable
5-10	Low Plasticity	With Clay	Plastic
10-20	Medium	Silt + Clay	Not acceptable
20-35	High	Silty + Clayey)	) Plastically) compressible)
>35	Very high	Clayey)	)

Apparatus:

○ Spatula
○ Liquid Limit device with grooving tool *(TRRL, 1974) see* Fig. 4.

- ○ Sample containers
- ○ Balance: Sensitivity ± 0.01 gm
- ○ Wash bottle

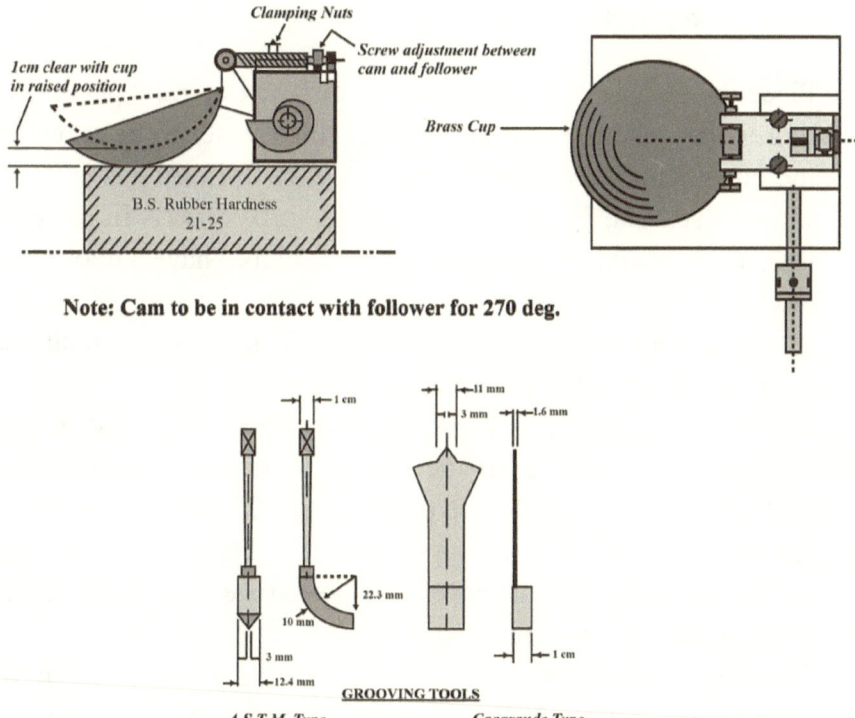

Figure 4. A Liquid Limit Device and Tools

Preparation of Test Sample:

- ○ Allow the soil sample to air drying
- ○ Break up the aggregates in the mortar using a pestle with rubber pad.
- ○ Select a representative sample by quartering or riffling
- ○ Separate the test sample by sieving on U.S. No. 10 sieve. Grind those retained on No. 10 sieve, using mortar and rubber padded pestle, to have them broken into individual grain sizes and thereafter separate again on No. 10 sieve.

○ Collect all portions passing No. 10 sieve to separate on No. 40 sieve. Take a sample weighing about 100 gm from the material passing No. 40 sieve for the determination of Liquid Limit.

Test procedure:

○ Place the sample in the evaporating dish or flat glass plate. Mix thoroughly, using a spatula, with distilled water to be added in increments until the mass becomes a thick uniform paste.

○ Using a spatula, place a portion of the mixed mass in the cup, then squeeze and spread, and finally level it to have a maximum thickness of one inch (25.4 mm). Divide the soil, using the grooving tool with maximum of six firm strokes, along the diameter through the center of the hinge.

○ Lift and drop the cup by turning the crank at the rate of two revolutions per sec. until the two parts come into contact at bottom of the groove along a distance of 1/2 inch (12.5 mm).

○ Record the number of blows and take a slice of soil from the portion of the sample that have just flowed together, in a container to determine the moisture content.

○ Transfer all soil remaining in the cup to be mixed with soil in the evaporation dish or flat glass plate. Wipe the cup and grooving tool dry.

○ Repeat the foregoing steps at least four times with the same sample but each time adding distilled water to increase moisture content. It is desired that the number of blows shall be within 35 and 15.

Calculations:

○ Determine the moisture content of each test specimen.

○ Draw a flow curve representing the relationship between moisture content and the corresponding number of blows on a semi-Log chart with the former as ordinate on plain scale and the latter as abscissa on the Logarithmic scale. DRAW THE BEST FITTING STRAIGHT LINE.

Reporting:

○ Determine the moisture content corresponding to the intersection of the flow curve, with the 25 blows abscissa and report it as Liquid Limit) of the soil.

○ Report
  * Method of sample drying
  * Percent passing US # 40 sieve w_p
  * Apparatus used

○ FOR EXTREMELY SANDY SOILS, TRY PLASTIC LIMIT (w_p) BEFORE LIQUID LIMIT (w_L) TEST. IF (w_L) CANNOT BE DETERMINED, REPORT (w_p) AS NON-PLASTIC.

2.3   DETERMINATION OF PLASTIC LIMIT OF SOILS

Scope:

This test covers the determination of the lowest moisture content at which the soil will behave as plastic material.

Apparatus:

○ Evaporating dish or flat glass plate (500 mm square).
○ Spatula
○ Surface for rolling
○ Moisture content containers
○ Balance: Sensitivity 0.01 gm.

Preparation of Test Sample:

○ Same as stated for Liquid Limit test
○ Take 15-20 gm of the specimen mass

Test Procedure:

○ Place the air dried sample in an evaporating dish or flat glass plate to thoroughly mix up with distilled water in increments to make a homogenous mass which should be plastic enough to be easily shaped into a ball.

○ Take about 8 to 10 gm of the sample. Roll this mass, as shown in (Fig. 5) between the fingers and glass plate (placed on a smooth horizontal surface) with just sufficient pressure to form a thread of uniform diameter *(Teng, 1962)*.

○ When the diameter of the thread becomes 3.2 mm (1/8 inch), break it and squeeze together between thumb and fingers into a uniform mass. Try rolling again into a thread of the said diameter. REPEAT THIS PROCEDURE UNTIL THE THREAD START JUST CRUMBLING WHEN IT HAS BEEN ROLLED INTO A THREAD OF 3.2 MM DIAMETER:

○ Collect the portions of crumbled soil together and place in a container with its lid on. REPEAT THE ABOVE PROCEDURE 2-3 TIMES.

Calculations:

○ Determine the moisture content of the soil in each of the container sand report the average value as Plastic Limit (w_p) IF THE VALUE OF (w_p) DIFFERS BY MORE THAN 1% THE TEST SHOULD BE REPEATED.

Reporting:

○ Report the Plastic Limit (w_p) to the nearest whole number
○ When Plastic Limit cannot be determined, report it as Non-

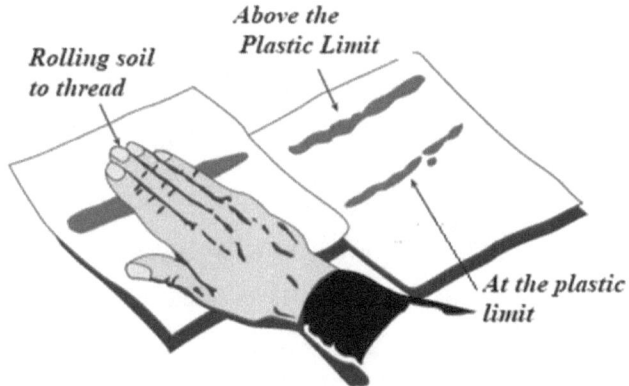

Figure 5. Determination of Plastic Limit

Plastic (NP).

○ WHEN BOTH LIQUID LIMIT (W_L) AND PLASTIC LIMIT ARE DETERMINED, EVALUATE VALUE OF PLASTICITY INDEX (I_p) USING EQUATION (2). REPORT THE SOIL AS NON-PLASIC WHEN THE VALUE IS ZERO OR NAGATIVE OR WHEN EITHER OR BOTH (W_L) AND (W_p) CANNOT BE DETERMINED.

2.4 DETERMINATION OF LINEAR SHRINKAGE OF SOILS

Scope:

○ This test covers the determination of the linear shrinkage of dried soil specimen as a percentage of its original length.

Apparatus:

○ Semi-cylindrical brass (or other non-corrodible metal) mould of 140 mm long and 25 mm diameter.
○ Flat glass plate of 500 mm square, 10 mm thick with beveled edges and rounded corners.

- ○ Spatula
- ○ Silicone grease
- ○ Vanier caliper: 0.1 mm accuracy and over 150 mm range.
- ○ Sample containers

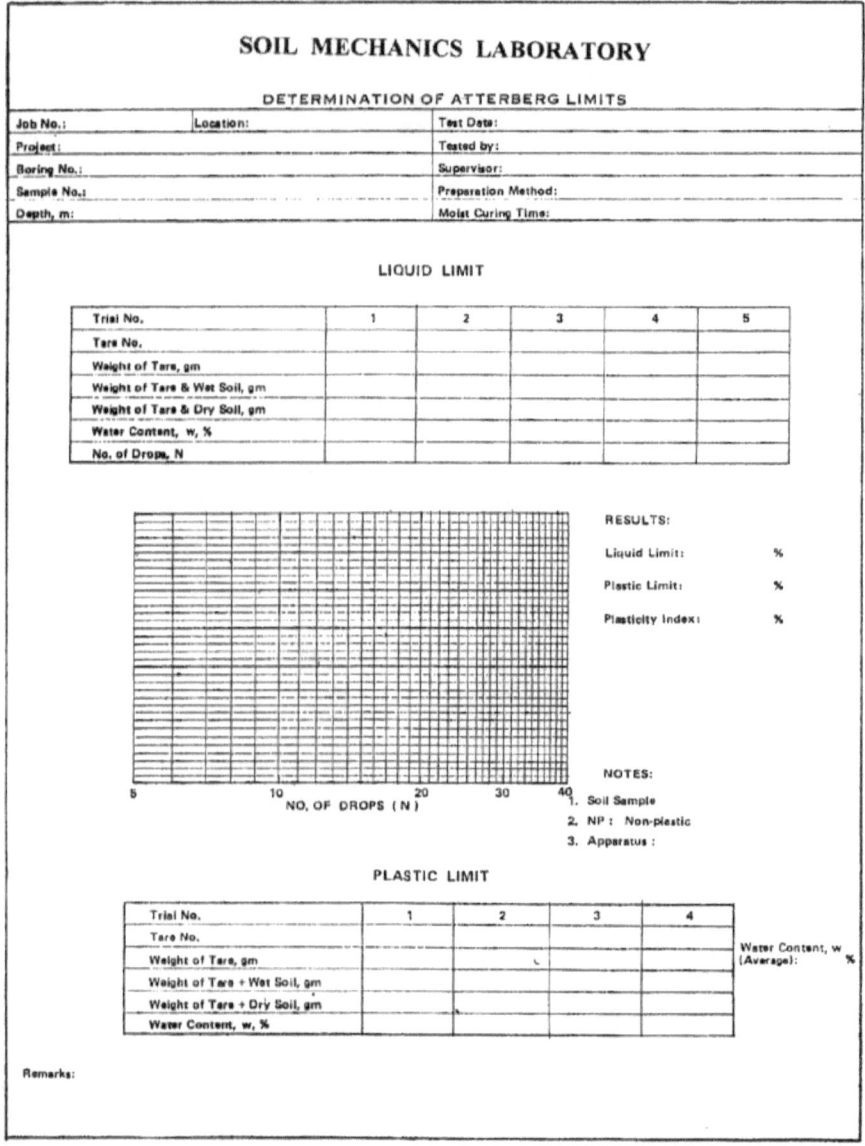

SOIL MECHANICS LABORATORY

DETERMINATION OF ATTERBERG LIMITS

Job No.:	Location:	Test Date:
Project:		Tested by:
Boring No.:		Supervisor:
Sample No.:		Preparation Method:
Depth, m:		Moist Curing Time:

LIQUID LIMIT

Trial No.	1	2	3	4	5
Tare No.					
Weight of Tare, gm					
Weight of Tare & Wet Soil, gm					
Weight of Tare & Dry Soil, gm					
Water Content, w, %					
No. of Drops, N					

RESULTS:

Liquid Limit: %

Plastic Limit: %

Plasticity Index: %

NO. OF DROPS (N)

NOTES:

1. Soil Sample
2. NP : Non-plastic
3. Apparatus :

PLASTIC LIMIT

Trial No.	1	2	3	4
Tare No.				
Weight of Tare, gm				
Weight of Tare + Wet Soil, gm				
Weight of Tare + Dry Soil, gm				
Water Content, w, %				

Water Content, w (Average):   %

Remarks:

Preparation of Test sample:

○ Similar to Liquid Limit (W_L) test
○ Take about 150 gm of the specimen mass

Test Procedure:

○ Place the specimen mass on the glass plate. Add water in small increments to mix the sample thoroughly until a smooth homogenous paste at about the Liquid Limit is obtained.
○ Place the paste in the mould which has been cleaned and greased thinly to the inner surface. Overfill the mould slightly with the soil paste avoiding the inclusion of air pockets and tap it gently on the bench.
○ Level off the mould top with the spatula and remove the excess soil from the rim of the mould.
○ Leave the mould with soil exposed to draught-free area. When the soil has shrunk from the walls, place the mould in an oven maintained at 60-65°C. Increase temperature to 110±5°C when shrinkage has virtually ceased and maintain for 10-15 hours.
○ Allow mould and soil to cool down in a desiccator.
○ Measure the length of bar of soil with the vernier calipers. Take an average of 2 to 3 observations.

Calculations:

$$LS = \left(\frac{L_0 - L_D}{L_0} \right) \times 100 \tag{3}$$

Where:

LS = Linear Shrinkage in %
L_D = length of dry specimen, cm
L_0 = original length in cm (14 cm if a standard mould is used)

Reporting:

○ Linear Shrinkage to nearest whole number
○ Percentage of original sample passing 425 μ m sieve.

2.5 DETERMINATION OF PARTICLE SIZE DISTRIBUTION OF SOILS

Soils are composed of particles of various sizes occuring in different proportions which can be out into the following two major groups as in Table 2.

Grain size analysis is another routine test used to determine the ranges of particle sizes making up the soil mass, and also the distribution of particles sizes. Two principal methods are used- sieve and Combined Sieve and Hydrometer. The former method is adopted for coarse grained soils (>0.075 mm) while the later method is used

Table 2. Major Soil Groups (after ASTM, 1982, part 19, pp. 118 & 367-388)

Soil Group	Basic Reqmnt.	Soil Description	Particle size (mm)
I. Coarse Grained	More than 50% retained on U.S. sieve # 200	I. Gravels :Coarse grained :Fine grained	19.0-75.0 4.75-19.0
		II. Sand :Coarse sand :Medium sand :Fine sand	2.00-4.75 0.425-2.00 0.075-0.425
II. Fine Grained	More than 50% passing U.S sieve # 200	Silt and Clay	<0.075

when the soil contains grains of silt and clay size (<0.075 mm) to a considerable extent, at least 10% as specified in B.S. 1377 Test 7 (D). The grain size analyses are generally presented in the form of a chart.

A typical grain size chart is given in Fig. 6. (Bowles, 1970 p. 40) Grain sizes corresponding to10, 30 and 60% passing designated as, D_{10} D_{30} and D_{60} respectively) are determined from the chart to define the following:

I. Co-efficient of uniformity

$$C_u = \frac{D_{60}}{D_{10}} \qquad (4)$$

II. Co-efficient of curvature

$$C_z = \frac{(D_{30})^2}{D_{10} \times D_{60}} \qquad (5)$$

Project *University of Basra*   Job. No. *5*

Location of Project *Garmat Ali*   Boring No. *2*   Sample No. *3*

Description of Soil *Sand*   Depth of Sample *10 m.*

Tested By. *H.A.D*   Date of Testing *12/2/1975*

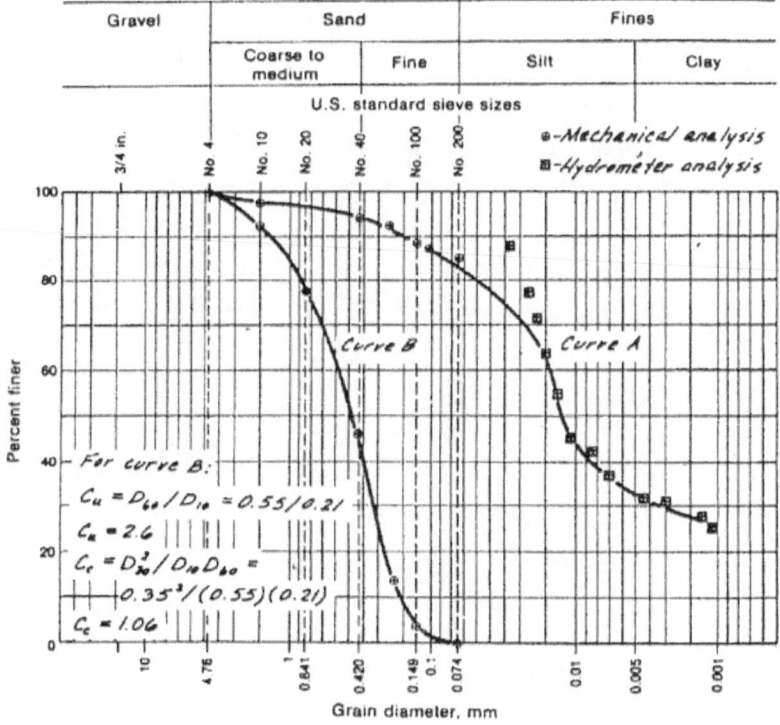

Figure 6. Typical Grain Size Distribution Curves

These values provide useful indication about the shape of the grain size curve and used for classification of a predominantly coarse grained soils.

2.5.1. SIEVE ANALYSIS METHOD FOR COARSE GRAINED SOILS

Scope:

This test covers the quantitative determination of the particle size distribution in a soil down to fine sand size (>0.075 mm). The fine fraction (silt and clay size particles) can be also evaluated.

The procedure involves separation of clay and silt sized particles (<0.075 mm) by wet sieving on U.S. No. 200 to be followed by dry sieving sieve of the remaining coarse grained material. This method is, therefore, satisfactory for cohesionless soils.

The separation of particles are accomplished by allowing the coarse fraction of the soil sample to pass through a nest of sieves (Fig. 7) and recording the mass of material retained on each sieve (Lambe, 1967, p. 30). These sieves are made of woven wire cloth with square openings or mesh and are available in sizes ranging between 125 mm and 0.038 mm (ASTM E-11 specification).

Apparatus:

○ Nest of sieves: A set of the following sieves confirming to **ASTM** Specification E-11 are required:

3 inch	(75 mm)
1 1/2 inch	(37.5 mm)
3/4 inch	(19.0 mm)
3/8 inch	(9.5 mm)
No. 4	(4.75 mm)
No. 10	(2.00 mm)
No. 16	(1.18 mm)
No. 40	(0.425 mm)

No. 100   (0.150 mm)

No. 200   (0.075 mm)

Pan

Sieve cover

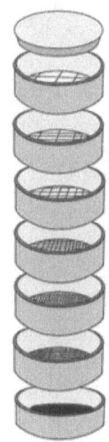

Figure 7. Sieves for Grain Size Analysis

- Balances: Accuracy ± 0.5 gm and 0.01 gm
- Sample Divider (Riffle box)
- Drying Oven: Thermostatically controlled for maintaining temperature of 110 ± 5°C.
- Scoop: 200 mm long and 100 mm wide
- Sieve brushes: Hair and Wire brushes
- Mechanical Sieve Shaker
- Mortar and pestle

Preparation of Test sample:

- Leave the sample for air drying
- Break up aggregations using mortar and rubber padded pestle.
- AVOID CRUSHING OF THE INDIVIDUAL PARTICLES.
- Mix the sample thoroughly and evenly
- Divide the sample by quartering or riffling

○ Oven dry the sample at $110 \pm 5°C$ and allow to cool down in a desiccator.

○ Take a representative mass of 400-500 gm of sample

Test procedure:

○ Place the sample in a porcelain dish, add water and leave for several hours

○ Transfer the sample in small quantities on U.S.# 200 sieve and then wash the material through the sieve using tap water until the water passing is clear. AVOID OVERLOADING THE SIEVE.

○ Collect the washed out material in a large pan and allow to settle down. Decant the clear water and put the mixture in the oven to dry out at $110 \pm 5°C$ for at least 16 hours. Determine the dry weight of this sample fraction.

○ Pour the residue by backwashing into a porcelain dish and allow the suspension to become clear. Decant the clear water and then place the dish with soil in the oven maintained at $110 \pm 5°C$ for at least 16 hours.

○ Weigh this oven dry sample fraction and pour it on the top of an orderly nested sieves (Top most one having largest opening). Set the sieve cover and pan respectively on top and bottom of the nest of sieves. Place the entirely assembly on a mechanical sieve shaker and operate it for 10 minutes.

○ Remove the stack of sieves from the shaker and obtain weight of material retained on each sieve.

○ SUM UP ALL THE FRACTIONS TO COMPARE WITH THE TOTAL WEIGHT OF SAMPLE POURED IN.

Calculations:

• Compute the percentage retained R (%) on each sieve as follows:

$$R\ (\%) = \frac{\text{Mass of dry soil retained on the sieve, } W_r}{\text{(Total mass of dry sample, WT)}}\ 100\% \qquad (6)$$

- Calculate the percentage passing (P%) on each sieve as follows:

$P(\%)$ $=$ 100 - cumulative percentage retained on the sieve, (R_{cum})

$=$ Percentage passing on the sieve immediately above $(P_{preceeding})$

- Percentage retained on the on the sieve, (R)　　　　**(7)**

- CHECK

$$W_T = W_P + W_R \tag{8}$$

$$W_R = \Sigma W_r \tag{9}$$

Where

W_T $=$ Total mass of dry sample, gm.

W_P $=$ Mass of sample fraction washed out, gm

W_R $=$ Mass of sample fraction retained on # 200 sieve during washing, gm

W_r $=$ Mass of sample fraction retained on individual sieve, gm

Reporting:

The report shall include:

○ Maximum size of particles, mm and D_{50}, mm
○ Percentage passing on each sieve in tabular form or presented by plotting on a Semi-Logarithmic graph.
○ Determine D_{50}, from the plot, mm and evaluate the values of (C_u) and (C_z) whenever applicable.

SOIL MECHANICS LABORATORY

GRAIN SIZE ANALYSIS — WET SIEVING METHOD

Job No. :	Location:		Test Date:
Project:		Tested by:	
Boring No.:		Supervisor:	
Sample No.:		Preparation Method:	
Depth of Sample, m:		Separation Sieve:	

A. BEFORE WASHING

Total Dry Sample, W_T, gm:

B. AFTER WASHING ON US # 200 SIEVE

Portion of Sample Retained, W_R, gm:

Portion of Sample Passing, W_p, gm:

FORMULAE:

1. Percent Retained (R) $= \dfrac{W_r}{W_T} \times 100$ ..... (%)

2. Percent Passing (P) $= 100 - R_{cum}$ ..... (%)

   $= P_{preceeding} - R$

3. $W_T = W_p + W_R$

   $= W_p + \Sigma W_r$ ..... (gm)

Sieve No.	Sieve Opening (mm)	Weight of Tare, gm	Weight of Soil + Tare, gm	Weight of Soil Retained, gm	Percent Retained	Cumulative Percent Retained	Percent Passing
				W_r	R	R_{cum}	P'
3 inch	75.0						
1½ inch	37.5						
¾ inch	19.0						
3/8 inch	9.5						
No. 4	4.75						
No. 10	2.00						
No. 16	1.18						
No. 40	0.425						
No. 100	0.150						
No. 200	0.075						
Pan							

$$\Sigma W_r =$$

Remarks :

2.5.2. SIEVE AND HYDROMETER ANALYSES FOR FINE AND VERY FINE GRAINED SOILS

Scope:

This test covers the quantitative determination of the distribution of particle sizes in soils completely using both sieve and hydrometer analysis. Sieve analysis is used for the determination of particle sizes of coarse fraction of the soil (particles larger than 75μm) while particle sizes for the fine fraction (particles smaller than 75μm) are determined by a sedimentation process using a hydrometer. This method is not applicable if less than 10% of the material passes the US Sieve No. 200 (75μm).

The sedimentation method utilizes the Stokes equation for the terminal velocity of a falling sphere in a liquid (Stokes, 1891). To obtain the velocity of fall of the particles, a hydrometer is used. Most commonly used hydrometer for soil testing is ASTM 152H type (Fig. 8). This particular type of hydrometer is calibrated to read grams of soil with G = 2.65 in 1000 ml of suspension.

Apparatus:

o Balances: Sensitivity: 0.01 gm (Hydrometer analysis)
                                   0.1% mass of sample (Sieve analysis).
o Hydrometer: ASTM Hydrometer 152H
o Sedimentation cylinder: Capacity 1000 cc
                                   ID Such that 1000 cc mark is 36 ±2 cm from inside bottom.
o Stirring apparatus: Electrical
o Thermometer: Capacity 0-50°C
o Sieves: A set of sieves conforming to ASTM Specification E-11 to include the following:

3 inch	(75 mm)	No. 10 (2.00 mm)
1 1/2 inch	(37.5 mm)	No. 16 (1.18 mm)

3/4 inch	(19.0 mm)	No. 40 (0.425 mm)
3/8 inch	(9.5 mm)	No.100 (0.150 mm)
No. 4	(4.75 mm)	No. 200 (0.075 mm)

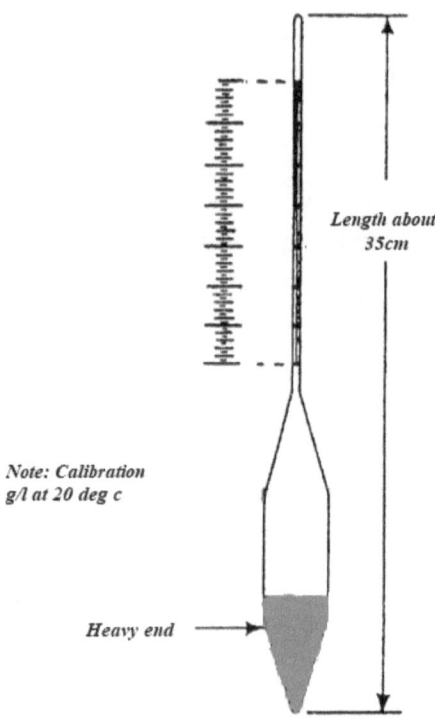

Length about 35cm

Note: Calibration g/l at 20 deg c

Heavy end ⟶

Figure. 8. Soil hydrometer

- ○ Water bath: Thermostatically controlled
- ○ Beaker
- ○ Stopwatch
- ○ Dispersing agent: Stock solution of Sodium Hexameta phosphate and distilled water (40 gm of chemical per litre of solution).

Preparation of Test Sample:

- ○ Expose the sample for air drying. Break up the aggregation of particle (if any) using mortar and rubber covered pestle.

- By quartering or riffling select a representative sample of the mass of 400-500 gm.
- Separate on U.S. No. 10 sieve. Set aside the portion passing and place the portion retained in a pan and add water to allow soaking for several hours until aggregations become soft.
- Place a pan below No. 10 sieve and wash the material. Crumble the lumps, if any, encountered.
- Dry the material retained at $110 \pm 5°C$ and separate on No. 10
- sieve. Add material passing with those similar material in Step III.
- Use the material retained in Step V for sieve analysis.
- Allow the washing material to settle for several hours, decant or siphon off clear water and dry the soil at 60°C. Using mortar and rubber pestle, disaggregate and then mix thoroughly with similar material from Step V. Take a representative portion of the material for hydrometer analysis by quartering. Approximate mass of material shall be

Sandy soil	- 100 gm
Silt and clay	- 50 gm

Test procedure:

a. **Sieve analysis of portion retained on No. 10 sieve:**
   Sieve the portion retained on No. 10 sieve using the following nest of sieves:
   3 inch (75 mm), 1 1/2 inch (37.5 mm), 3/4 inch (19.0 mm), 3/8 inch (9.5 mm), No. 4 (4.75 mm) and No. 10 (2.00 mm). Place the set of sieves in order with 3 inch (75 mm) sieve on the top. Use mechanical sieve shaker to shake 15 minutes.

b. **Hydrometer analysis of portion passing No. 10 sieve**
   - Take a representative sample of the following mass:

Sandy soils	- 100 gm
Silt and clay	- 50 gm

- Place the sample in 250 cc beaker and add to it 125 cc of stock dispersing solution (40 gm/litre). Stir the mixture and allow for soaking at least for 16 hours.
- Transfer all the soil-water slurry into the dispersion cup by washing with distilled water.
- ENSURE THAT NO RESIDUE IS LEFT IN THE BEAKER.
- Place the cup in the stirring device and stir for 10 minutes to disperse the particle completely. Immediately after dispersion, transfer all the material using distilled water to the sedimentation cylinder. Add distilled water until the volume is 1000 cc.
- Using the palm of the hand over the open end of the cylinder agitate the soil suspension for at least one minute. Set the jar on the table and take observations by inserting hydrometer at the following elapsed time: 2, 5, 15, 30, 60, 250 and 1440 minutes. After each observation, carefully remove the hydrometer and place it with a spinning motion in a graduated cylinder filled with clean distilled water. Record the temperature at the end of each hydrometer reading.
- At the end of final reading, transfer the suspension to No.
- 200 sieve to wash with water until it is clear. Dry the portion retained at 110+5°C and make sieve analysis on it.

c. **Determination of Composite Correction C_{comp} for Hydrometer Reading.**

- Prepare 1000 cc of liquid composed of distilled water and 125 cc of stock dispersing agent (Sodium Hexameta- phosphate) solution @ 40 gm/litre.
- Place the liquid in a sedimentation cylinder and the cylinder in the constant temperature bath.
- Set for at least two constant temperatures (expected during the observations) of the liquid, insert the hydrometer and take the readings at the top of the meniscus formed on the stem of

the hydrometer. For hydrometer ASTM 152H the composite correction is the difference between the reading and zero.

○ Use of interpolation to obtain the composite correction for any intermediate temperature and preferably prepare a table for various temperatures.

○ Record the meniscus correction, (C_m)

Calculations:

a. Sieve Analysis Values for Portion Coarser than No. 10 Sieves

○ Percentage retained on individual sieve

$$= \frac{\text{Mass retained on each sieve}}{\text{Total mass of soil sample, } W_T} \qquad \text{(10)}$$

○ Percentage passing each sieve

$$= \% \text{ Passing on the sieve immediately above} \qquad \text{(11)}$$
$$- \% \text{ retained on the sieve}$$

b. Sieve Analysis Values for Portion Finer than No. 10 Sieve

○ **WEIGHTED MASS OF SAMPLE, (W)**

$$= \frac{\text{Mass of oven dry sample taken for Hydrometer analysis } W_H}{\text{Fraction Passing No. 10 sieve}} \qquad \text{(12)}$$

○ **Percentage retained on individual sieve**

$$= \frac{\text{Mass retained on the seive}}{\text{Weighted mass of sample W}} \qquad \text{(13)}$$

○ **Percentage passing each sieve**

$$= \% \text{ Passing on the sieve immediately above (14)}$$
$$= \% \text{ retained on the sieve}$$

c. Hydrometer analysis

• Effective diameter of soil particles:

$$D = K \sqrt{(L_{eff}/t)} \tag{15}$$

Where

D	=	diameter of particle, mm
L_{eff}	=	Effective depth (Table-3, take $R = (R_a + C_m)$
K	=	constant dependent on temperature of the suspension and specific gravity of soil particle (Table 4)
t	=	elapsed time in minutes
R_a	=	hydrometer reading in the soil suspension at the top of meniscus
C_m	=	meniscus correction

* Values of effective depth are calculated from the equation (16):

$$L = L_1 + {}^1/_2 \{L_2 - (V_B/A)\} \tag{16}$$

Where:

L	=	effective depth, cm,
L_1	=	distance along the stem of the hydrometer from the top of the bulb to the mark for a hydrometer reading, cm,
L_2	=	overall length of the hydrometer bulb, cm,
V_B	=	volume of hydrometer bulb, cm³, and
A	=	cross-sectional area of sedimentation cylinder, cm²

Values used in calculating the values in Table 2 are as follows: For both hydrometers, 152H:

$$L_2 \quad = \quad 14.0 \text{ cm}$$

$$V_B = 67.0 \text{ cm}^3$$
$$A = 27.8 \text{ cm}^2$$

For hydrometer 152H:

$$L_1 = 10.5 \text{ cm for a reading of 0 g/litre}$$
$$= 2.3 \text{ cm for a reading of 50 g/litre}$$

Table 3. Values of Effective Depth Based on Hydrometer and Sedimentation Cylinder of Specified Sizes (ASTM 1982, Part 2)

Hydrometer 152H			
Actual Hydrometer Reading	Effective Depth L cm.	Actual Hydrometer Reading	Effective Depth L cm.
0	16.3	31	11.2
1	16.1	32	11.1
2	16.0	33	10.9
3	15.8	34	10.7
4	15.6	35	10.6
5	15.5		
6	15.3	36	10.4
7	15.2	37	10.2
8	15.0	38	10.1
9	14.8	39	9.9
10	14.7	40	9.7
11	14.5	41	9.6
12	14.3	42	9.4
13	14.2	43	9.2
14	14.0	44	9.1
15	13.8	45	8.9
.16	13.7	46	8.8
17	13.5	47	8.6
18	13.3	48	8.4
19	13.2	49	8.3
20	13.0	50	8.1
21	12.9	51	7.9
22	12.7	52	7.8
23	12.5	53	7.6
24	12.4	54	7.4
25	12.2	55	7.3
26	12.0	56	7.1
27	11.9	57	7.0
28	11.7	58	6.8
29	11.5	59	6.6
30	11.4	60	6.5

Table 4. Values of K for Use in Equation for Computing Diameter of Particles in Hydrometer Analysis (after ASTM D422, Part 19, 1982, p. 120)

Temperature deg C	Specific Gravity of Soil Particles								
	2.45	2.50	2.55	2.60	2.65	2.70	2.75	2.80	2.85
16	0.01510	0.01505	0.01481	0.01457	0.01435	0.0141	0.01394	0.01374	0.01356
17	0.01511	0.01486	0.01462	0.01439	0.01417	0.0139	0.01376	0.01356	0.01338
18	0.01492	0.01467	0.01443	0.01421	0.01399	0.0137	0.01359	0.01339	0.01321
19	0.01474	0.01449	0.01425	0.01403	0.01382	0.0136	0.01342	0.01323	0.01305
20	0.01456	0.01431	0.01408	0.01386	0.01365	0.0134	0.01325	0.01307	0.01289
21	0.01438	0.01414	0.01391	0.01369	0.01348	0.01328	0.01309	0.01291	0.01273
22	0.01421	0.01397	0.01374	0.01353	0.01332	0.01312	0.01294	0.01276	0.01258
23	0.01404	0.01381	0.01358	0.01337	0.01317	0.01297	0.01279	0.01261	0.01243
24	0.01388	0.01365	0.01342	0.01321	0.01301	0.01282	0.01264	0.01246	0.01229
25	0.01372	0.01349	0.01327	0.01306	0.01286	0.01267	0.01249	0.01232	0.01215
26	0.01357	0.01334	0.01312	0.01291	0.01272	0.01253	0.01235	0.01218	0.01201
27	0.01342	0.01319	0.01297	0.01277	0.01258	0.01239	0.01221	0.01204	0.01188
28	0.01327	0.01304	0.01283	0.01264	0.01244	0.01225	0.01208	0.01191	0.01175
29	0.01312	0.01290	0.01269	0.01249	0.01230	0.01212	0.01195	0.01178	0.01162
30	0.01298	0.01276	0.01256	0.01236	0.01217	0.01199	0.01182	0.01165	0.01149

○ Percentage of soil in suspension (percent finer or passing)

$$P = (R_c \times a / W) \times 100 \qquad (17)$$

Where

a	=	correction factor from Table 5
R_c	=	hydrometer reading after composite correction applied
	=	hydrometer reading in the soil suspension at the top of meniscus, R_a - hydrometer reading evaluated for the dispersing agent solution at the same temperature, from (Table 6)
W	=	weighted mass of sample, gm

Table 5. Values of Correction Factor, a, for
Different Specific Gravities of Soil Particles"
(after ASTM D422, 1982 part 19, p. 112)

Specific Gravity	Correction Factor[a]
2.95	0.94
2.90	0.95
2.85	0.96
2.80	0.97
2.75	0.98
2.70	0.99
2.65	1.00
2.55	1.01
2.50	1.03
2.45	1.05

[a] For use in equation for percentage of soil remaining in suspension when using Hydrometer 152H.

Table 6. Calibrated Values for Composite Correction (Hydrometer: 152H)

Temperature, °C	Composite Correction, C_{comp}
15	5.5
16	5.2
17	4.9
18	4.6
19	4.4
20	4.1
21	3.8
22	3.6
23	3.4
24	3.1
25	2.9
26	2.6
27	2.4
28	2.1
29	1.8
30	1.5

Note: All specifications conform to ASTM D-422

Reporting:

○ Present the results in graphical form on a chart in which particle diameters are plotted as abscissa on a logarithmic scale and the corresponding percentage passing plotted as ordinates to an arithmetic scale.

○ Provide a description of the soil

○ Report the dispersing agent and dispersion period.

SOIL MECHANICS LABORATORY

GRAIN SIZE ANALYSIS — SIEVE & HYDROMETER METHOD

Job No.:	Location:		Test Date:
Project:		Specimen Preparation Method:	Dry / Wet
Boring No.:		Separation Sieve: U.S. Sieve #10	
Sample No.:		Tested by:	
Depth of Sample:		Supervisor:	

TOTAL OVEN DRY SAMPLE, W_T, gm:

FOR HYDROMETER OVEN DRY SAMPLE, W_H, gm:

Hydrometer ASTM 152H	No.:
	Jar No.:
Dispersing Agent	Type: Sodium Metaphosphate
	% : 4 (40 gm/litre)
Specific Gravity	G_s:
	Factor a :
Correction	Meniscus, cm, Unit: 1

HYDROMETER ASTM 152H:

$L_1 \cong 10.5$ cm for R = 0
$\cong 2.3$ cm for R = 50
$L_2 \cong 14$ cm
$V_b \cong 67$ cm^3
$A = 27.8$ cm^2

FORMULAE:

1. W, gm $= W_H /$ Percent Passing No. 10 Sieve
2. $R = R_a + C_m$
3. L_{eff} (cm) $= L_1 + \frac{1}{2}(L_2 - V_b/A)$
4. D (mm) $= K\sqrt{L_{eff}/t}$
5. $R_c = R_a - C_{comp}$
6. $a = G_s (1.65)/(G_s - 1)(2.65)$
7. P (%) $= (R_c \times a/w) \times 100$

SIEVE ANALYSIS					HYDROMETER ANALYSIS										
	U.S. Sieve	Retained		Passing %	Date/Time (t_o Hrs)	Elapsed Time, t, min.	Temp., °C	Actual Hydr. Reading, R_a	Hydr. Reading, R	L_{eff}, cm	K	$\sqrt{L_{eff}/t}$	Particle Diam. D, mm	Comp. Corr. C_{comp}	Corr. Hydr. Reading, R_c	Percent Passing P, %
		gm	%													
PORTION OF SAMPLE RETAINED ON #10 SIEVE [USE W_T, gm]	¾″															
	3/8″					2										
	# 4					5										
	#10															
PORTION OF SAMPLE PASSING ON #10 SIEVE [USE W, gm]	#10					15										
	#16					30										
	#40					60										
	#100															
	#200					1440										
	Pan															

Remarks:

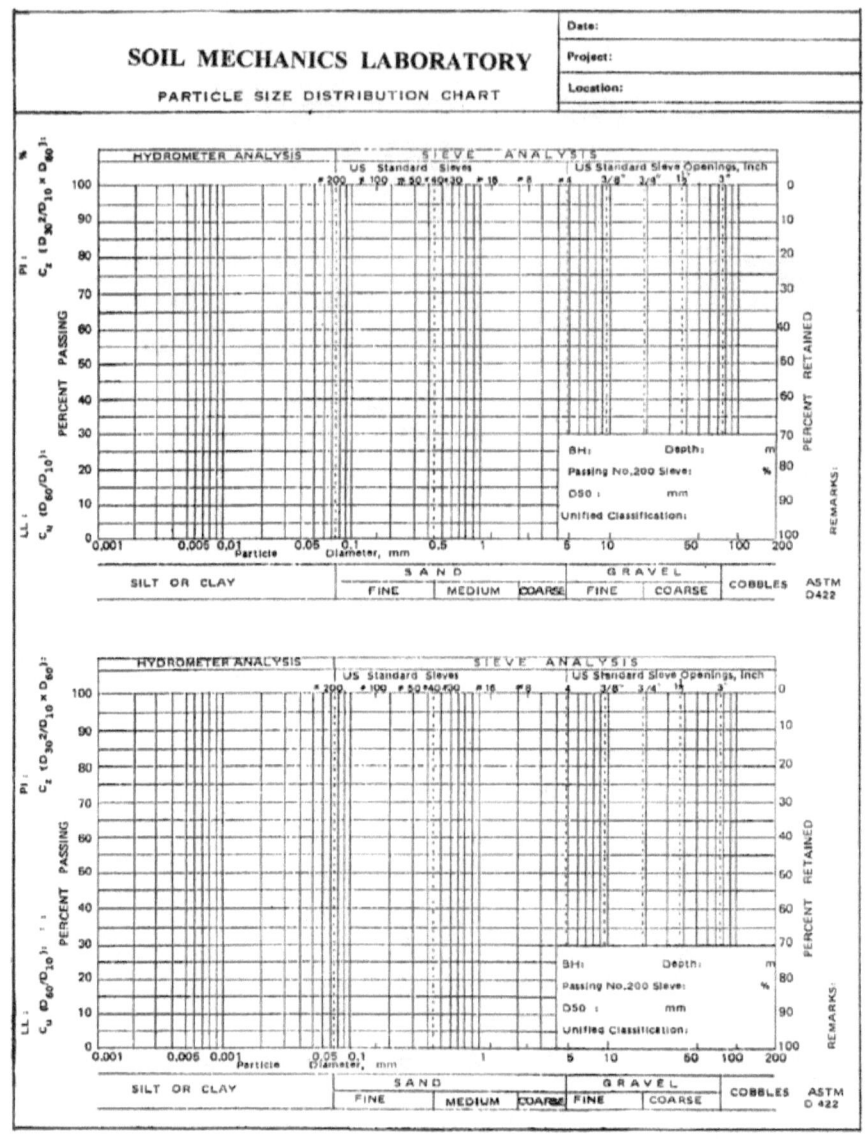

2.6 DETERMINATION OF SPECIFIC GRAVITY OF SOIL SOLIDS

Scope:

This test covers the determination of the specific gravity of soil solids by means of a density bottle. By specific gravity of a soil it is meant the average value for all the soil grains composing the mass of it.

Specific gravity of soil has got a number of direct applications:

○ Computation of most laboratory testing:
   Hydrometer analysis, Determination of void ratio of a soil etc.
○ Identification of soil minerals:
   Iron minerals have a much higher value of specific gravity while Peat has a very low value of specific gravity. The usual range of specific gravity values are given in Table 7.

Table 7. Typical values of specific Gravity of
Soil Solids (after Bowles 1970, p.56)

Type of soil	G_S
Sand	2.65 − 2.67
Silty sand	2.67 − 2.70
Inorganic clay	2.70 − 2.80
Soils with micas or iron	2.75 − 3.00
Organic soils	Variables but may be under 2.00

Apparatus:

○ Density bottles: Capacity 50 ml with stopper (Required 3 bottles)
○ Constant temperature water bath
○ Vacuum desiccator
○ Oven: Thermostatically controlled at 110 ±5°C
○ Sample containers
○ Balance: Sensitivity 0.001 gm
○ Small riffle box

- Vacuum source and tubing or heating device
- Chattaway spatula (3 x 150 mm)
- Wash bottle and rubber gloves
- De-aired distilled water

Preparation of Test Sample:

- Quarter the original sample to 50-100 gm specimen
- Gravel size particles, if present, must be ground to pass U.S. No. 10 sieve
- Dry in oven at 105-110°C then cool in a desiccator
- Riffle sample to obtain a 30 gm specimen

Test Procedure:

- Clean each density bottle, dry in oven, cool in desiccator and weigh to the nearest 0.001g*m*.
- Fill the bottle with de-aired distilled water to the top and immerse in a constant temperature bath. Remove the bottle from the water bath after one hour, insert the stopper carefully, wipe outside with a clean and dry cloth. Take the weight of bottle with water to nearest 0.001 gm and note down the temperature of water in degrees Celsius (T_i °C).
- Divide prepared specimen into 3 parts and place each in a density bottle. Weigh each bottle with soil to nearest 0.001 gm.
- Add de-aired distilled water to soil until bottles are half full.
- Remove entrapped air by boiling gently for at least 30 minutes while intermittently shaking it to assist the expulsion of all the air or by applying vacuum.
- When de-airing process is complete, cool the hot bottles containing samples (if applicable) to room temperature.
- Fill the bottles to top with de-aired distilled water, insert stopper and place in constant temp bath for at least 1 hour.

○ Remove bottles from bath, insert stoppers, dry quickly with a clean and dry cloth, and weigh to nearest 0.001 gm. Note down the temperature of the contents in ° c ($.T_x$ °c).

Calculations:

Calculate the specific gravity G_S of soil solids as follows:

$$G_s \text{ (at } T_x) = \frac{W_o}{W_o + W_a(\text{at } T_x) - W_b(\text{at } T_x)} \qquad (18)$$

and

$$W_a \text{ at } (T_x) = \frac{\gamma_w(\text{at } T_x)}{\gamma_w(\text{at } T_i)} [W_a(\text{at } T_i) - W_f] + W_f \qquad (19)$$

where

W_O	=	Weight of sample of oven dry soil, gm
$W_{a(\text{at } T_i)}$	=	Weight of bottle + water at temperature T_x °c gm
$W_{b(\text{at } T_x)}$	=	Weight of bottle + Water + Soil at temperature T_x °cw gm
W_f	=	Weight of bottle, gm
γ_w	=	Relative Density of water

$$G_{s(\text{at } 20°)} = K \times G_{s(\text{at } T_{xo})} \qquad (20)$$

(Values of γ_w and κ are given in Table 8)

Table 8. Relative Density of Water and Conversion Factor K For Various Temperatures (after ASTM, 1982, part 19, p.214)

Temperature, deg C	Relative Density of Water	Correction Factor K
18	0.9986244	1.0004
19	0.9984347	1.0002
20	0.9982343	1.0000
21	0.9980233	0.9998
22	0.9978019	0.9996
23	0.9975702	0.9993
24	0.9973286	0.9991
25	0.9970770	0.9989
26	0.9968156	0.9986
27	0.9965451	0.9983
28	0.9962652	0.9980
29	0.9959761	0.9977
30	0.9956780	0.9974

Reporting:

The specific gravity is reported to the nearest 0.01 as the average of three values. If one values differs from average by more than 0.03, repeat test. Report the liquid other than water if used.

SOIL MECHANICS LABORATORY

DETERMINATION OF SPECIFIC GRAVITY OF SOIL SOLIDS

JOB NO. :	TEST DATE :	
LOCATION :	PROJECT :	
BORING NO. :	SAMPLE DESCRIPTION:	
SAMPLE NO. :	METHOD OF AIR REMOVAL:	
SAMPLE DEPTH, m :	TESTED BY:	SUPERVISOR:

	WEIGHT IN GM, OF					SPECIFIC GRAVITY OF SOIL SOLIDS	SPECIFIC GRAVITY OF SOIL SOLIDS
FLASK	FLASK + WATER	FLASK + WATER + SOIL	OVEN DRY SOIL	FLASK + WATER	WATER		
W_f	W_a $T_i = \ldots °C$	W_b $T_x = \ldots °C$	W_o	W_a $T_x = \ldots °C$	W_w $T_x = \ldots °C$	G_s $T_x = \ldots °C$	G_s $T = 20°C$

FORMULAE:

1. $W_{a(at\ T_x)} = \dfrac{T_w\ at\ T_x}{T_w\ at\ T_i}\ (W_{a(at\ T_i)} - W_f) + W_f$

2. $W_w = W_a + W_{a(at\ T_x)} - W_{b(at\ T_x)}$

3. $G_{s(at\ T_x)} = \dfrac{W_o}{W_w}$

4. $G_{s(at\ 20°C)} = K \times G_{s(at\ T_x)}$

TABLE   Relative Density of Water and Conversion Factor K For Various Temperatures

Temperature, deg C	Relative Density of Water	Correction Factor K
18	0.9986244	1.0004
19	0.9984347	1.0002
20	0.9982343	1.0000
21	0.9980233	0.9998
22	0.9978019	0.9996
23	0.9975702	0.9993
24	0.9973286	0.9991
25	0.9970770	0.9989
26	0.9968156	0.9986
27	0.9965451	0.9983
28	0.9962652	0.9980
29	0.9959761	0.9977
30	0.9956760	0.9974

REMARKS: _____

_____

---

3. SOIL STRENGTH TESTS

These tests aim at determining a very important property of soils called the 'Shear Strength'. The shear strength defined as the maximum shearing resistance offered by the soil to an applied external applied load: It is made up of two components.

○ **Friction:** due to interlocking of particles and also friction between particles

○ **Cohesion:** due to internal forces holding the soil particles together in solid mass.

Three principal methods are adopted to determine the shear strength of soil in the laboratory: Direct Shear, Unconfined Compression and Triaxial Compression. Because of the fact that shear strength is related to condition prevailing in situ and can vary with time, it cannot be considered as a unique property of soil. The choice of a particular method should be based on how close the test condition simulating the realistic at the field under existing and anticipated condition.

3.1   DETERMINATION OF UNCONFINED COMPRESSIVE STRENGTH OF SOILS

Scope:

This test covers the determination of the Unconfined Compressive Strength of cohesive soil in the undisturbed condition using strain controlled application of the load.

The unconfined compressive strength is defined as the maximum axial load per unit area or that at 20% axial strain whichever occurs first.

Unconfined compression is the simplest and quickest method to measure the approximate shear strength of cohesive soils but its main limitation is that it cannot simulate the confinement state of soil.

Apparatus:

o Compression machine: 20 kN capacity
o Sample extruder
o Dial gauges
o Vernier caliper: Sensitivity 0.25 mm
o Stop watch
o Drying oven: Thermostatic controlled for 110± 5°C
o Balances: Sensitivity 0.01 gm for mass up to 100 gm Sensitivity 0.1 gm when mass above 100 gm
o Miscellaneous apparatus
o Specimen trimming device
o Moisture content containers

Preparation of Specimen:

o Specimen dimension
   Minimum diameter: 1.3 inch (33 mm)
   Height/Diameter ratio: 2 to 3
o Preparation
   - Cut a portion from large sample such that it is 25% oversize in dimension.
   - Trim it carefully to the diameter of the specimen. MAKE SURE THAT THE SPECIMENS ARE OF UNIFORM CIRCULAR CROSS-SECTION.
   - Square the ends using split specimen holder such that they are perpendicular to the longitudinal axis.

o Place the specimen in the compression machine. ENSURE THAT IT IS PROPERLY ALIGNED.
o Sample description

- ○ Bring the upper platen just in contact with the specimen and set the load and deformation measuring dials preferably at zero at initial condition.
- ○ Apply load to produce axial strain at a strain controlled rate of 1/2 to 2% per minute and record the load every 30 sec. or any convenient interval.
- ○ Continue loading until 20% of strain is attained. Record the load and corresponding deformation dial reading.

Calculations:

- For any load, calculate axial strain ϵ

$$\epsilon\ (\%) = \frac{\Delta H}{H_o} \tag{21}$$

Where

ΔH = Change in height of the specimen, cm
H_0 = initial height of the specimen, cm

- The average cross-sectional area for an instantaneous applied

$$A\ (cm^2) = \frac{A_0}{1 - \frac{\epsilon}{100}} \tag{22}$$

Where

ϵ = Instantaneous axial strain, %
A_o = Initial cross-sectional area, cm^2

- Axial Stress (load per unit area) for an instantaneous applied load

$$\sigma_1(kPa) = \frac{P}{A} \times 98.1 \tag{23}$$

Where:

P = Applied load, kg
A = Corresponding average x-sectional area, cm^2

Reporting:

- ○ Type and dimension of the specimen
- ○ Initial moisture content, density and degree of saturation
- ○ Plot showing the relationship between axial stress and axial strain with stress as ordinate and strain as abscissa
- ○ Report the maximum stress or stress corresponding to 20% axial strain
- ○ Make a sketch of the test specimen at failure condition

SOIL MECHANICS LABORATORY

UNCONFINED COMPRESSION TEST

Job No.:	Project:		Test Date:
Boring No.:		Location:	
Sample No.:	Sample Description:		
Sample Depth, m:	Specimens: D_0(cm):	H_0(cm):	A_0(cm^2):
Proving Ring No.:	C:	kg/Div, Rate of Strain:	mm/Div, Tested by:

Deformation Dial Reading mm	Load Dial Reading (Units)	Sample Deformation, (cm)	Axial Strain, (%)	Area Corr. Factor	Corrected Area (cm^2)	Load, (kg)	Axial Stress, kPa
PR		ΔH	ϵ	CF	A	P	σ_1

1. $\epsilon = \dfrac{\Delta H}{H_0} \times 100$ (%)   **Failure Sketch**   Remarks:

2. $CF = 1 - \dfrac{\epsilon}{100}$

3. $A = \dfrac{A_0}{CF}$ (cm^2)

4. $P = PR \times C$ (kg)

5. $\sigma_1 = \dfrac{P}{A} \times 98.1$ kPa

3.2 DETERMINATION OF STRENGTH PARAMETERS OF SOIL IN TRIAXIAL COMPRESSION

Scope:

This test covers the determination of shear strength of preconsolidated undisturbed cylindrical soil specimens tested in Undrained Triaxial Compression with pore water pressure measurement (Bishop and Henkel, 1962 after Thornton and Welch 1975).

Triaxial test (Fig. 9) can provide for allowing drianage if required to simulate the in situ and that anticipated in future in the field, and can also take care for confinement state of soil. It is thus suited for all types of soil provided that the proper specimen is obtainable. The state of stresses under triaxial compression during shearing is illustrated in Fig. 10.

The test method involves

○ placing cylindrical specimen of undisturbed soil which is encased in a rubber membrane in a trixial compression cell
○ subjecting it to cell and back pressures (the former being slightly higher)
○ allowing for consolidation under a certain confining pressure
○ loading axially under strain controlled condition, to quick failure (Allowing no drainage during shear)
○ recording Pore Water Pressure developments -

A minimum of 3 specimens are required to establish the strength envelope for a soil.

The shear strength is defined as the maximum deviator stress or that at 20% shear strain whichever occurs first.

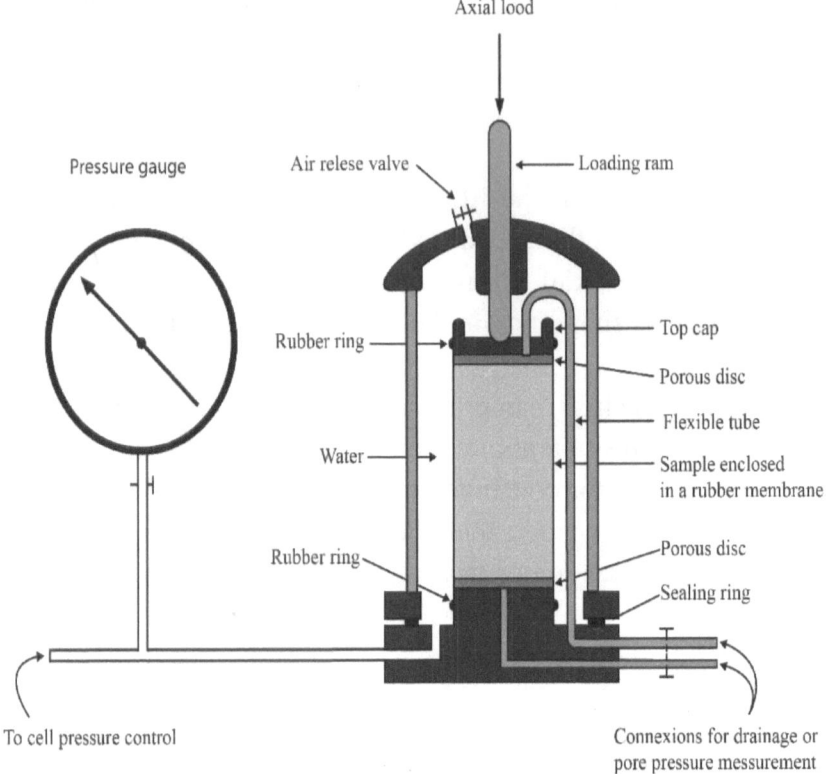

Figure 9. Diagrammatic layout of the triaxial test

Equipment:

- Triaxial Cell
- Compression machine
- Specimen caps and bases
- Rubber membranes and O rings
- Vacuum pump and pressure units (for loose soil)
- Specimen trimmer
- Proving Ring
- Deformation measuring gauges
- Proving Ring
- Volume change indicator
- Balances
- De-aired water

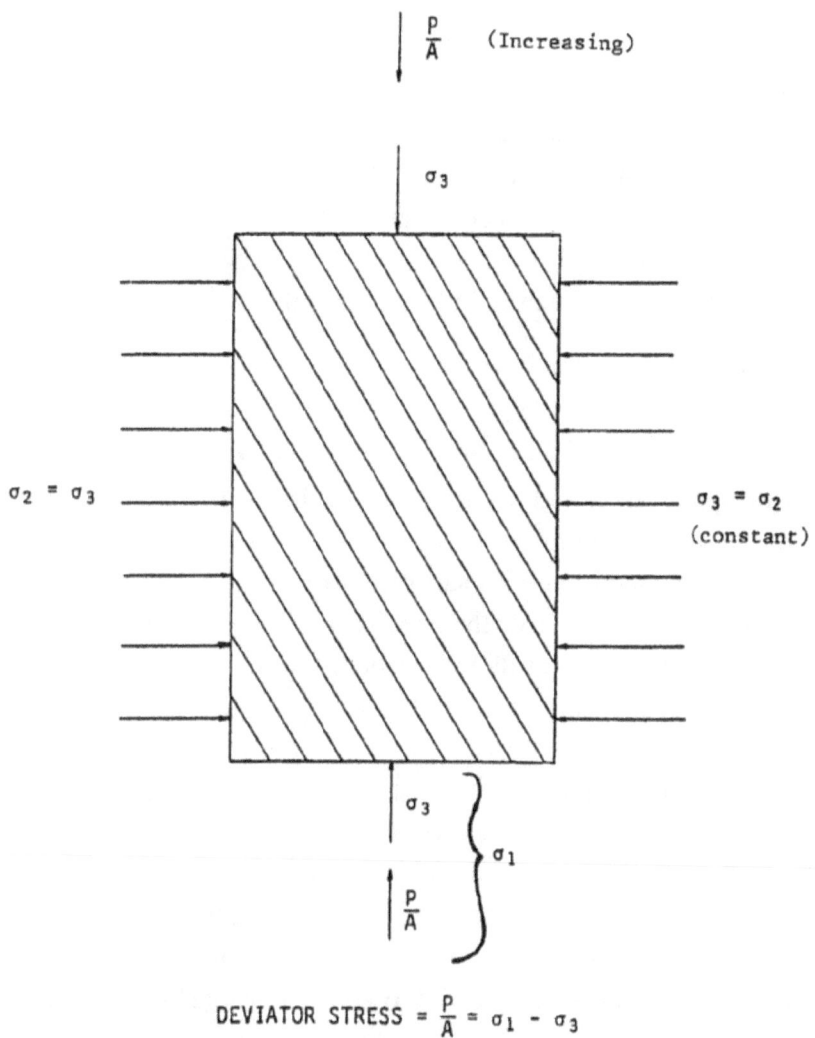

$$\text{DEVIATOR STRESS} = \frac{P}{A} = \sigma_1 - \sigma_3$$

Figure 10. State of stress during Trixial Testing

Preparation of Specimen:

○ Dimension

- Standard specimen diameter 1.4 inch (35 mm)
- Height to Diameter Ratio, 1:2

Procedure

○ Take a 25% oversize section of suitable length from the undisturbed sample and trim specimen to the required diameter. Cut the specimen to the required length using a cradle.
○ Take soil trimmings to conduct moisture content determination
○ Measure the height and diameter of the specimen and take the weight to determine the bulk unit weight.

Test Procedure:

○ Place the specimen, so prepared, in the triaxial cell base. Use filter paper disk and porous stone of the same diameter between the base and specimen.
○ Wrap the specimen with saturated filter paper strips and place a rubber membrane over the specimen using membrane stretcher.
○ Cap the specimen at its top, stretch the membrane at both ends and fasten the membrane with O-rings to the cap or top platen and base platen.
○ Keeping drainage line closed, set a predetermined pressure, usually 30 Psi (207 kPa) to both the chamber and pore water pressure lines. Using the hand pump increase in small increments both the cell and back pressure simultaneously. When they attain 30 Psi (207 kPa) provide direct corrections to constant pressure device. Increase cell pressure to attain 31 Psi (214 kPa) and leave the sample for at least 16 hours to achieve saturation.
○ Keeping back pressure constant, increase the cell pressure to attain the desired confinement and then allow for consolidation for 24 hours. Record the change in volume during consolidation.
○ Shear the specimen by increasing off the drainage line and then increasing the axial load at a controlled strain rate of 5% per hour. Record the pore water pressure developments during shearing. REPEAT OPERATION FOR AT LEAST 2 MORE SPECIMENS. CHOOSE THEINTERMEDIATE CONFINING PRESSURE SAME AS IN-SITU.

Calculations:.

○ Calculate corrected cross-sectional area

A_C (cm^2) as follows:

$$A_C = \frac{V_c}{H_0 - \Delta H_C} = \frac{V_0 - \Delta V}{H_0 - \Delta H_C} \tag{24}$$

where

V_0 = initial volume of specimen, cm^3

ΔV = change in volume due to consolidation, cm^3

ΔH_C = change in height due to consolidation, cm (assumed $\Delta H_C = 0$)

H_o = initial height of specimen, cm

○ Calculate the deviator stress $\sigma_1 - \sigma_3$ as follows:

$$\sigma_1 - \sigma_3 \text{(kPa)} = \frac{\text{Load}}{\text{Area}} = \frac{PR \times C}{A_i} \times 98.1 \tag{25}$$

where

$$A_i = \frac{A_c}{1 - \epsilon/100} = \frac{V_c}{H_i} \tag{26}$$

where

A_i = Instantaneous cross-sectional area of specimen, cm^2

c = Proving Ring Constant, kg/div.

PR = Proving Ring reading

ϵ (%) = Axial strain = $\dfrac{\Delta H}{H_O} \times 100$ \hfill (27)

H_i = Instantaneous height of specimen, cm

ΔH = Change in light of the specimen, cm

Reporting:

○ Plot the deviator($\sigma_1 - \sigma_3$) vs. Axial strain relationship (Fig11) Plot the change in pore water pressure (Δu) vs. shear strain relationship as suggested by (U.S. Army, 1970 after Welch& Thornton, 1977)

○ Draw Mohr stress circles using effective stresses and then draw tangent to all the Mohr's circles (Fig. 12) to determine the strength parameters, c_u ', and ϕ_u '. (Fig. 13).

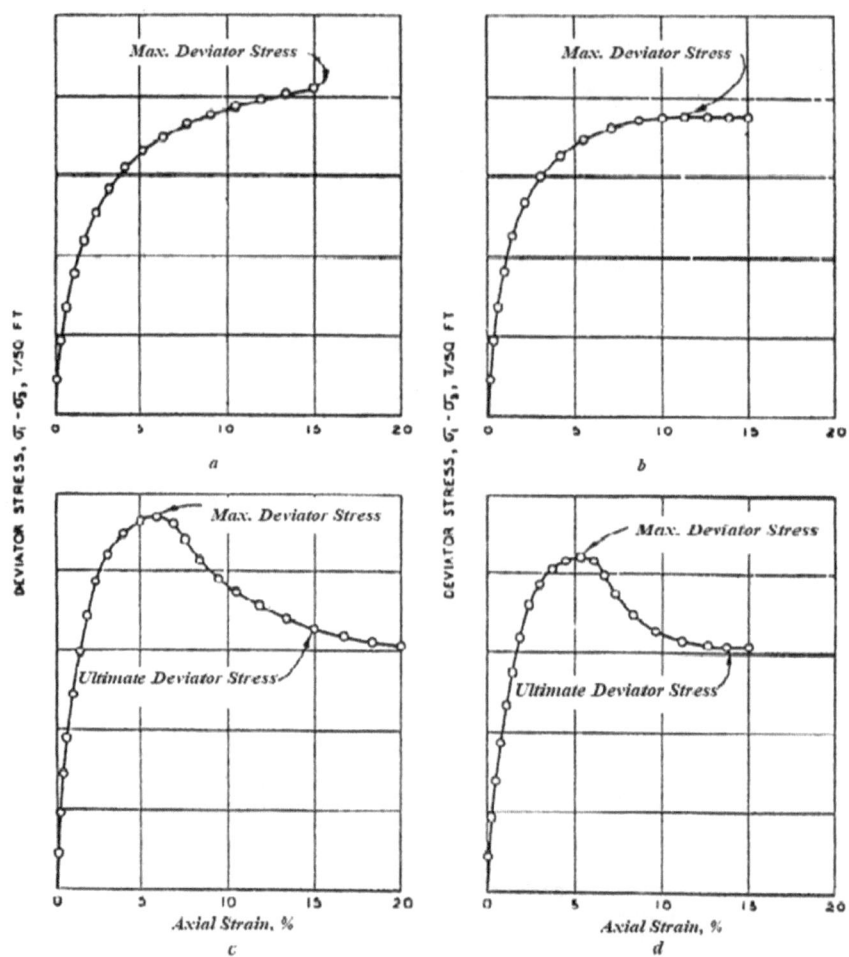

Figure 11. Typical stress-strain curves

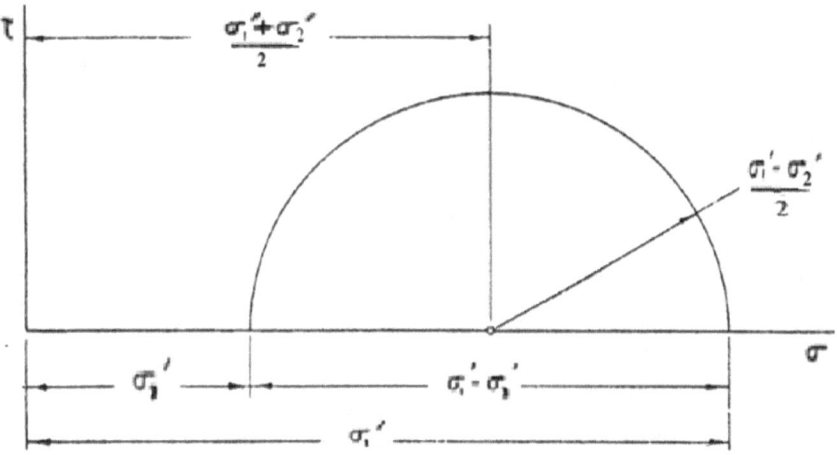

Figure 12. Construction for Mohr's Circle of Stress

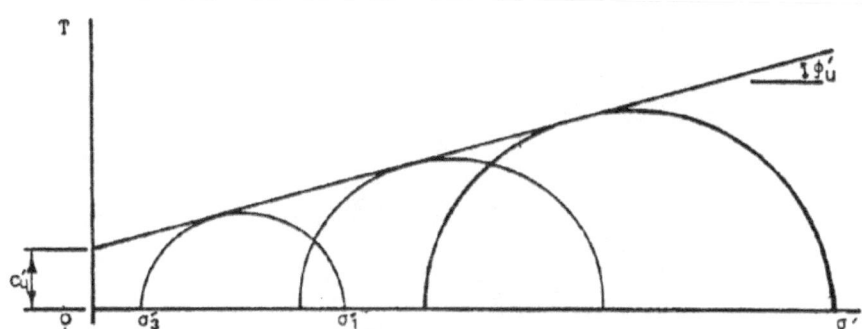

Figure 13. Construction of the CU strength envelope

SOIL MECHANICS LABORATORY

CONSOLIDATED UNDRAINED (CIU) TRIAXIAL TEST

Job No.:		Specimen D_o:	cm; H_o		cm; V_o:		cm^3	Test No.:	
Project:			G_s:		W_o		%	Test date:	
Boring No.:		Bulk Unit Weight, γ_b:					kg/m^3	Tested by:	
Sample No.:	Depth:	m	LL:	% PL:		%	Cell pressure, σ_3:		kPa
Description:		Rate of Strain:				mm/min	Back pressure, u:		kPa
Proving Ring No.:	e:	kg V_c:	After consolidation: cc	ΔV: A_c:		cc cm2	Consolidation pressure, σ_c:		kPa

READING Deformation (mm)	Load	Pore Water Pressure, kPa	Deformation (cm)	Height (cm)	Axial Strain, (%)	Corrected Area, cm^2	Load (kg)	Deviator Stress, kPa	Change in P.W.P., kPa
	PR	u_i	Δ_H	H_i	ϵ	A_i	P	$\sigma_1 - \sigma_3$	Δu

FORMULAE:

1. $A_c = \dfrac{V_o}{H_o} = \dfrac{V_o - \Delta V}{H_o}$ (cm^2)

2. $\epsilon = \dfrac{\Delta H}{H_o} \times 100 = \dfrac{H_o - H_i}{H_o} \times 100$ (%)

3. $A_i = \dfrac{V_o}{H_i} = \dfrac{1 - \epsilon/100}{A_c}$ (cm^2)

4. $\sigma_1 - \sigma_3 = \dfrac{P}{A_i} = \dfrac{PR \times e}{A_i} \times 98.1$ (kPa)

FAILURE SKETCH

REMARKS:

50

3.3 DETERMINATION OF STRENGTH PARAMETERS OF SOIL IN DIRECT SHEAR

Scope:

This test covers the determination of Shear Strength of undisturbed soils in direct shear.

In direct shear box (Welch & Thornton, 1977) as in (Fig. 14) popularly known as Shear Box Test, the soil is forced is to shear along a pre-determined plane. There is no control of drainage hence this can only be used to measure the shear strength of a soil under drained condition.

The test method involves:

○ placing a soil specimen in the horizontally splitting direct shear device
○ subjecting the specimen to predetermined vertical or normal stress
○ applying a horizontal or shearing force at a predetermined strain rate to the upper frame (Lower frame remain stationary) to fail the specimen along the splitting plane.

A minimum of three specimens are required to obtain the shear strength parameter.

Apparatus:

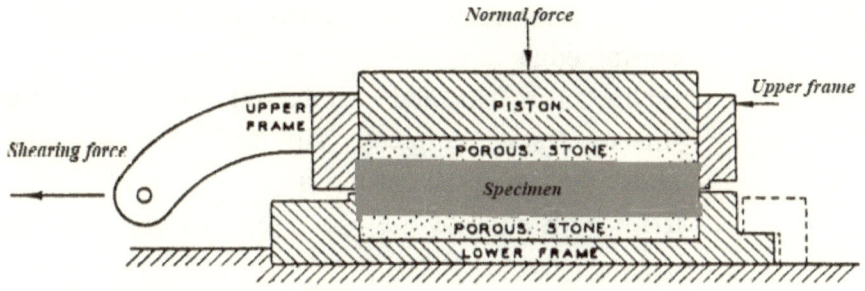

Figure. 14. Schematic diagram of direct shear box

- ○ Shear device
- ○ Porous stones
- ○ Normal force device
- ○ Horizontal force device
- ○ Dial gauges for displacement measurement
- ○ Sample trimmer
- ○ Balance 0.1 gm or 0.1% of specimen mass
- ○ Sample containers
- ○ Miscellaneous
  - • Knives
  - • Wire saw
  - • Distilled water
  - • Spatula

Preparation of Specimen:

- • **Specimen dimension**
  - ○ Minimum diameter or width: 50 mm
  - ○ Minimum thickness: 12.5 mm
  - ○ Minimum diameter/thickness: 2

- • **Procedure**

  - ○ Trim a portion of sample at least 1/2 inch (12.5 mm) larger in diameter and 1 inch (25.0 mm) greater in thickness than the specimen cutting ring.
  - ○ Take weight of the cutting ring and place with its cutting edge on top of specimen. Gently apply force on the cutting ring and trim the soil around. Continue this until soil completely fills and even protrudes above the top of the cutting ring.
  - ○ Trim both ends of the specimen to flush with the cutting ring.
  - ○ Record all data to conduct moisture content and bulk density determination.

Test Procedure:

○ Assemble the shear box with the upper and lower frames aligned and lock in position. APPLY THIN COATING OF LUBRICATION BETWEEN THE FRAMES.

○ Place a porous stone on the base plate of the shear box in the bottom of the lower frame. Carefully insert the specimen and place a porous stone on the top of it. Place the piston on the porous stone.

○ Place the shear box in position and connect the loading devices.

○ Position the displacement gauges and take the initial reading (set all gauges at zero if possible).

○ Apply the desired normal load gently on the specimen.

○ Shear the specimen at a constant lateral deformation of 0.03 to 0.04 inch/min (0.75 - 1.00 mm/min). Record the vertical deformation and the lateral load observations.

Calculations:.

○ Calculate initial and final moisture content, initial dry density, void ratio and degree of saturation.

○ Shear stress σ (kPa) $= \dfrac{\text{shear load}}{A} = \dfrac{PR \times C}{A} \times 98.1$ (28)

where

PR	=	Proving ring dial reading
C	=	Proving ring constant, kg/Div.
A	=	X-sectional area of the specimen, cm^2

Reporting:

○ Record initial moisture content, dry density, void ratio and degree of saturation

○ Plot the Shear Stress vs. Horizontal deformation for each specimen. As in (Fig. 15), (U.S. Army, 1970 after Welch & Thornton, 1977)

○ Plot vertical deformation vs. Horizontal deformation for each specimen

○   Plot the Maximum Shear Stress (τ max) vs. the Normal Stress (σ)

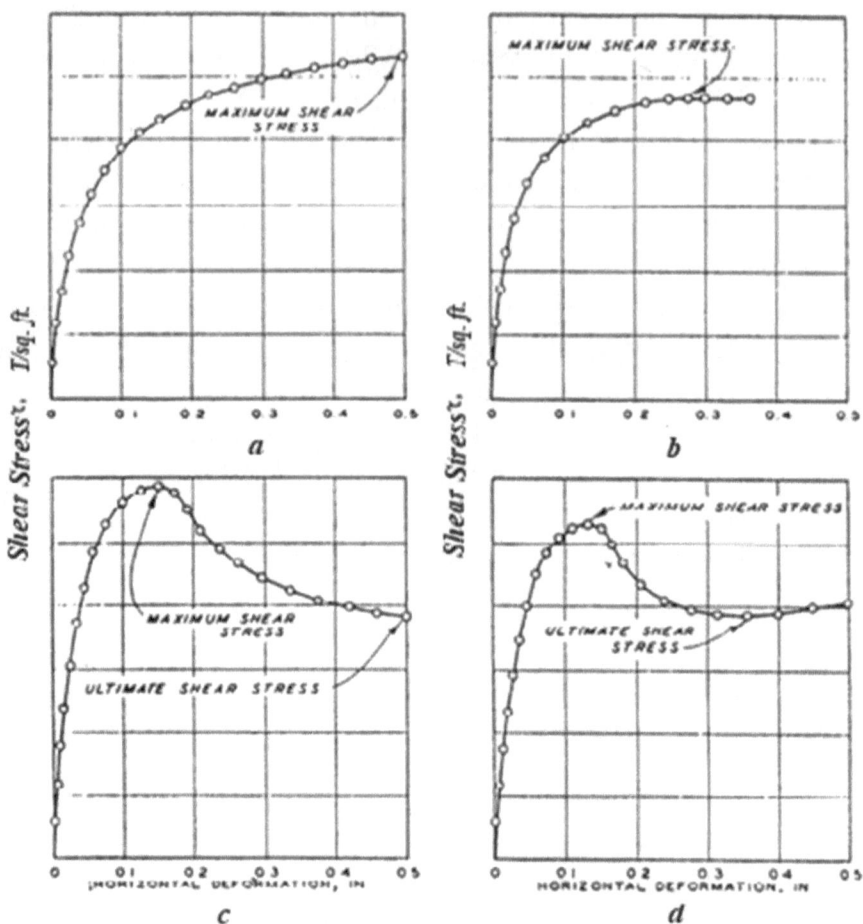

Figure15. Topical stress-deformation curves

for each specimen and draw a best fit straight line called 'Strength Envelope' for the soil. (Fig. 16)

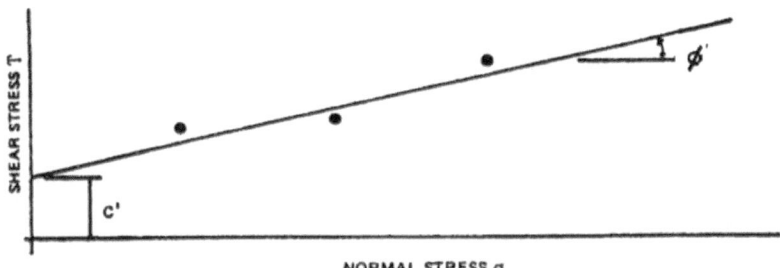

Figure 16. Construction of strength envelope

SOIL MECHANICS LABORATORY

DIRECT SHEAR TEST

Job No.:	Sample Description:	Test No.:
Location:	Specimen: D = cm ; H = cm; A = cm²	Test Date:
Boring No.:	Specific Gravity of Soil Solids, G̱ :	Tested By:
Sample No.	Water Table:	Supervisor:
Sample Depth, m:	Test Type:	Scale Load: + = kg
Proving Ring No.: Factor: kg/Div	Strain Rate: mm/min	Normal Stress: . kPa

HORIZONTAL DIAL READING ( )	VERTICAL DIAL READING ( )	PROVING RING READING	HORIZONTAL DISPLACEMENT, δ_h, mm	VERTICAL DISPLACEMENT, δ_v, mm	SHEAR LOAD, P, kg	SHEAR STRESS, τ, kPa

Formula: $\tau = \frac{P}{A} \times 98.1$ (kPa)

Remarks:

4. SOIL COMPRESSIBILITY TEST

4.1 DETERMINATION OF ONE DIMENSIONAL CONSOLIDATION PROPERTIES OF SOIL

Consolidation is a process of gradual transfer of an applied load from the pore water to soil structure as pore water is forced or squeezed out of the voids. This important fundamental phenomenon, first proposed by Austrian geologist K. Terzaghi in his classic consolidation Theory (Ca. 1925), got worldwide recognition because it helps to understand a particular soil behaviour in engineering problems called compressibility characteristics.

The laboratory consolidation test aims at obtaining soil data to be used in predicting the rate and amount of settlement of structure founded in clayey soils. This test also provide a method for a direct measurement of soils permeability.

Scope:

This method covers the determination of the magnitude and rate of consolidation of a saturated or near saturated specimen of soil.

A soil specimen in the form of a disc is completely confined laterally by a metal ring and then subjected to axial loading increments (Fig. 17). Two porous discs placed on the upper and lower faces of the specimen permit water to flow into or out of the soil. The deformation reading vs. elapsed time are recorded during each increment of loading. Each time, pressure is doubled and each constant pressure is maintained for 24 hours *(Welch & Thornton 1977)*.

Apparatus:

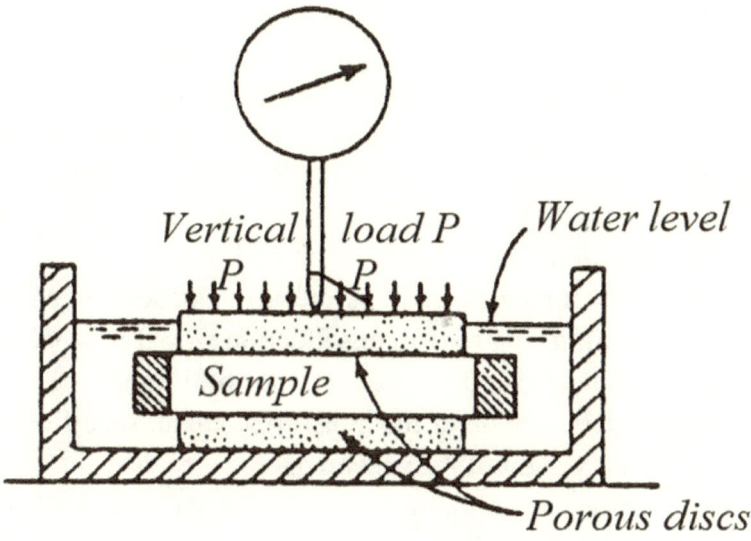

Figure 17. Schematic diagram of the consolidation test

○ Consolidometer
- Rigid base
- Porous stones
- Rigid load plate
- Consolidation ring: Minimum ID: 50 mm Minimum thickness: 1.25 cm Minimum diameter/thickness: 2.5 Inner surface to be coated with Teflon

○ Deformation indicator or dial gauge
○ Sample trimmer
○ Balance: Sensitivity 0.1 gm or 0.1% of sample weight (whichever smaller)
○ Oven: Thermostatically controlled to maintain $110 \pm 5°C$
○ Filter paper
○ Miscellaneous: Knives, wire saw, distilled water, moisture content containers, stop watch.

Preparation of the specimen:

○ Cut a portion from large sample and trim it such that it is 25% oversize in dimension

○ Place the cutting edge down on top of the trimmed sample and gently force the cutting ring into the sample. Trim the soil around the edge of the sample but with the loading edge of the cutting ring. Continue this until the soil completely fills and protrudes from the top of the cutting ring. Trim both surfaces of the sample to flush with the cutting ring. Carefully extrude the specimen from the cutting ring to the consolidation ring if it is necessary. Place two filter paper discs on each face of the specimen.

○ Conduct determination of the moisture content, specific gravity and, dry unit weight of the specimen.

○ Assemble the consolidometer. USE DAMPENED POROUS STONES ONLY.

Test Procedure:

○ Place the consolidometer containing the test specimen in the loading device and apply a seating load of 1 kPa to the specimen. Adjust the deformation dial gauge to take the initial reading and record it. (SETTING AT ZERO IS PREFERRED).

○ Place load on the consolidometer to obtain pressure on the specimen in increments with $\Delta p/p = 1$; a typical loading sequence is 12.5, 25, 50, 100, 200, 400, 800, 1600 kPa. THE FINAL PRESSURE MUST BE AT LEAST FOUR TIMES THE PRECONSOLIDATION PRESSURE.

○ Inundate the sample after the first load increment. Prevent specimen swelling by increasing loads unless it tends to swell under the estimated in situ vertical stress.

○ Maintain each pressure increment on the specimen for 24 hours and observe and record the deformation dial reading preferably according to the following elapsed time schedule: 0, 6, 9, 15 sec, 1, 2, 4, 8, 15, 30, 60, 120, 240 and 1440 minutes.

○ When rebound or unloading characteristics are desired, unload the specimen by pressure decrements in the reverse order. Maintain each rebound load on the specimen at least until the deformation dial gauge are constant with time.

○ Remove the specimen and the ring from the consolidometer and wipe the free water, oven dry the sample specimen and record the dry weight to obtain the dry mass of solid and the final moisture content.

Calculations:.

○ Height of soil solids, $H_s(cm) = \dfrac{W_d}{G_s \, \gamma_w A}$ 　　　　　　　(29)

　　　where
　　　　　　W_d = Dry weight of cylindrical specimen, gm
　　　　　　G_s = sp. gr. of soil solids
　　　　　　γ_w = unit weight of water = 1 gm/cc
　　　　　　A = Cross-sectional area of consolidation ring, cm^2

○ Void ratio, $e = \dfrac{H_i}{H_s} - 1$ 　　　　　　　　　　　　(30)

　　　Where
　　　　　　H_i= Instantaneous Height of specimen, cm

○ Strain, $\epsilon\,(\%) = \dfrac{\Delta H}{H_{preceeding}} \times 100 = \dfrac{\Delta H}{H_{i-1}} \times 100$ 　　　(31)

○ Co-efficient of volume compressibility, $m_v\,(m^2/kN) = \dfrac{\epsilon/100}{\Delta p}$ 　(32)

○ For each load increment, apply the Square Root of Time fitting method (Fig. 18) to the deformation vs. elapsed time data and calculate the co-efficient of consolidation, C_v as follows:

$$C_v(m^2/yr) = 0.848 \left[\left(\frac{\bar{H}}{2}\right)^2\right]\left(\frac{1}{t_{90}}\right) \times 52.56$$

　　　　　　　　　　　　　　　　　　　　　　　　　　(33)

　　　where
　　　　　　C_v 　= 　co-efficient of consolidation, m^2/yr
　　　　　　$\bar{H}$ 　= 　Mean sample thickness, cm
　　　　　　t_{90} 　= 　time for 90% consolidation, minutes

○ 　Use Casagrande method (Fig. 19) to determine preconsolidation pressure, p_c

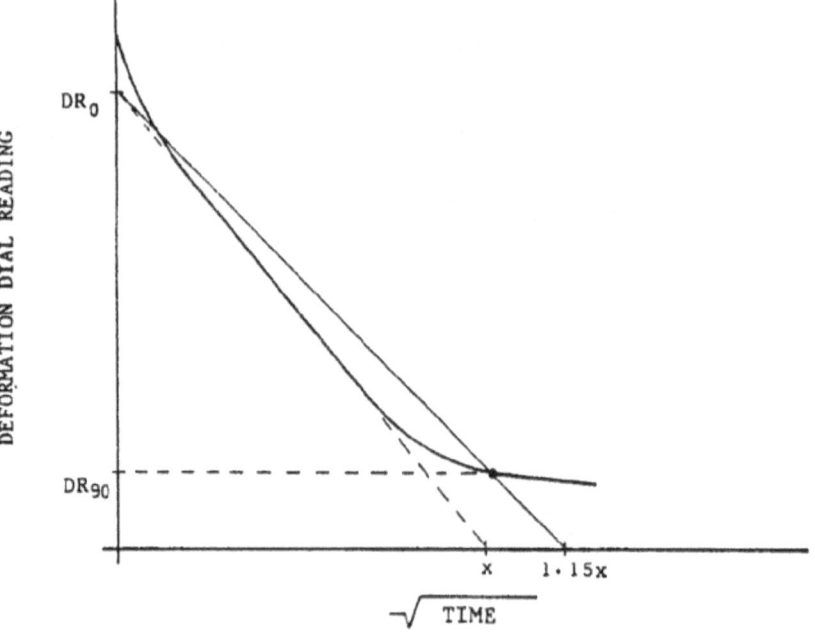

**Figure. 18. Graphical construction for
determining DR_0 and DR_{90}.**

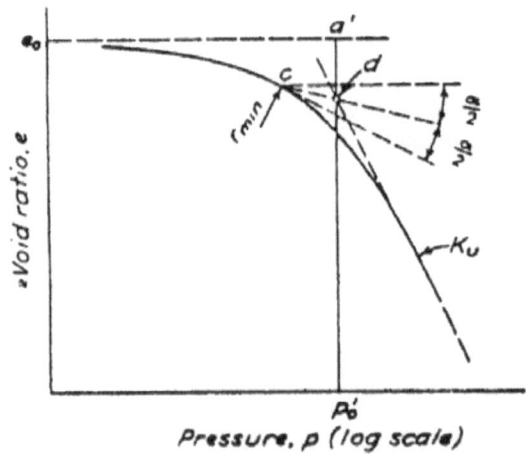

**Figure 19. Graphical construction for determining
former maximum pressure P, from the e-log curve**

Reporting:

The report shall include

- ○ Identification and description of sample
- ○ Initial and final moisture contents, dry unit weights and percentages of saturation

SOIL MECHANICS LABORATORY

CONSOLIDATION TEST

Job No.:	Location:		Dates of Test:		
Project:			Machine No. & Type:	/	Floating Ring / Fixed Ring
Boring No.:	Depth of Sample, m:		Tested by:		
Classification:	X-sec Area, A (cm²):		Water Content, w (%)	Initial	Final
Sp. Gr. of Soil Solids, G_s:	Height, H_0 (cm):		Bulk Unit Wt., γ_b(kg/m³)		
Liquid Limit (%):	Dry Weight, w_d (gm):		Void Ratio, e		
Plastic Limit (%):	Solid Height, H_s (cm):		Saturation, Sr (%)		

Loading Condition	Pressure, kPa		Settlement, ΔH, cm	Height, H_i (cm)	Mean Height, $\bar{H}$ (cm)	Strain, ε (%)	Co-eff. of Vol. Compr. m_v, m²/kN	Volume Ratio, f	Void Ratio, e
	p	Δp							

Pressure, p, kPa	Mean Pressure p, kPa $\sqrt{P_{n-1} \times P_n}$	t_{90} min	Co-eff. of Consolid^n. c_v, m²/yr.	Co-eff. of Permeality: k, m/yr.	Remarks:

FORMULAE:

1. $H_s = w_d/G_s\gamma_w A$ .... (cm)

2. $\varepsilon = \Delta H/H_{i-1} \times 100$ .... (%)

3. $m_v = \dfrac{\varepsilon/100}{\Delta p}$ ....(m²/kN)

4. $f = H_i/H_s$

5. $e = f - 1$

6. $Sr. = \dfrac{G_s \cdot w}{e} \times 100$ (%)

7. $c_v = \dfrac{0.848 \ (H/2)^2}{t_{90}} \times 52.56$ .... (m²/yr)

8. $k = c_v \cdot m_v \cdot \gamma_w = 10 \ c_v \cdot m_v$ ....(m/yr)

○ Pre-consolidation pressure
○ Plots of void ratio vs. Log of pressure and coefficient of consolidation vs. Log of average pressure

SOIL MECHANICS LABORATORY

CONSOLIDATION TEST — DATA SHEET

Job No.:	Location:		Dates of Test:	
Project:			Machine No. & Type:	/ Floating Ring / Fixed Ring
BH No.:	Depth of Sample, m:		Tested by:	

RING NO.				WEIGHT OF			Water Content, w, %	Bulk Unit Weight, γ_b, kg/m³
Height, H_o cm	Diameter, D, cm	X-sec. Area, A, cm²	Condition	Ring, gm	Wet Soil + Ring, gm	Dry Soil, gm		
			Initial					
			Final					

Press: kPa	Press: kPa	Press: kPa	Press: kPa	Press: kPa	Press: kPa
Date:	Date:	Date:	Date:	Date:	Date:
Time:	Time:	Time:	Time:	Time:	Time:
Temp. °C:	Temp. °C:	Temp. °C:	Temp. °C:	Temp. °C:	Temp. °C:

't'	Reading	't'	Reading	't'	Reading	't'	Reading	't'	Reading	't'	Reading
0 sec		0 sec		0 sec		0 sec		0 sec		0 sec	
5		5		5		5		5		5	
10		10		10		10		10		10	
15		15		15		15		15		15	
20		20		20		20		20		20	
30		30		30		30		30		30	
40		40		40		40		40		40	
1 min		1 min		1 min		1 min		1 min		1 min	
1.5		1.5		1.5		1.5		1.5		1.5	
2		2		2		2		2		2	
4		4		4		4		4		4	
9		9		9		9		9		9	
16		16		16		16		16		16	
36		36		36		36		36		36	
64		64		64		64		64		64	
2 hour		2 hour		2 hour		2 hour		2 hour		2 hour	

ΔH (cm):   ΔH (cm):   ΔH (cm):   ΔH (cm):   ΔH (cm):   ΔH (cm):

Press: kPa	Press: kPa	Press: kPa	Press: kPa	Press: kPa	Press: kPa
Date:	Date:	Date:	Date:	Date:	Date:
Time:	Time:	Time:	Time:	Time:	Time:
Temp. °C:	Temp. °C:	Temp. °C:	Temp. °C:	Temp. °C:	Temp. °C:

't'		't'		't'		't'		't'		't'	
0 sec		0 sec		0 sec		0 sec		0 sec		0 sec	
5		5		5		5		5		5	
10		10		10		10		10		10	
15		15		15		15		15		15	
20		20		20		20		20		20	
30		30		30		30		30		30	
40		40		40		40		40		40	
1 min		1 min		1 min		1 min		1 min		1 min	
1.5		1.5		1.5		1.5		1.5		1.5	
2		2		2		2		2		2	
4		4		4		4		4		4	
9		9		9		9		9		9	
16		16		16		16		16		16	
36		36		36		36		36		36	
64		64		64		64		64		64	
2 hour		2 hour		2 hour		2 hour		2 hour		2 hour	

ΔH (cm):   ΔH (cm):   ΔH (cm):   ΔH (cm):   ΔH (cm):   ΔH (cm):

5. SOIL PERMEABILITY TEST

5.1 DETERMINATION OF CO-EFFICIENT OF PERMEABILITY OF A SOIL BY THE FALLING HEAD METHOD

The permeability tests are performed directly on the undisturbed samples. Water is passed through the soil sample under variable hydraulic gradient. Darcy's law (Ca. 1856) for flow of fluid through porous media is applied for computation of the co-efficient of Permeability. The classification of soils based on degree of permeability is given in Table 9 (Terzaghi & Peck, 1948 after Head, 1982, part 2, p. 423), while the permeability and drainage behaviour of the principal soil types are indicated diagramatically in Fig. 20, (Bowles, 1980).

Table 9. Classification of Soil According to Permeability.

Degree of permeability	Range of coefficient of permeability, k (m/s)
High	Greater than 10^{-3}
Medium	$10^{-3} - 10^{-5}$
Low	$10^{-5} - 10^{-7}$
Very low	$10^{-7} - 10^{-9}$
Practically impermeable	Less than 10^{-9}

Scope:

This test outlines a method of determining the co-efficient of permeability of an undisturbed soil sample by the Falling Head Method, (Head, 1982) in Fig. 21. This method is suitable for measuring permeability of clays, silts and fine sands having co-efficient of Permeability varying from 10-4 to 10-10m/sec.

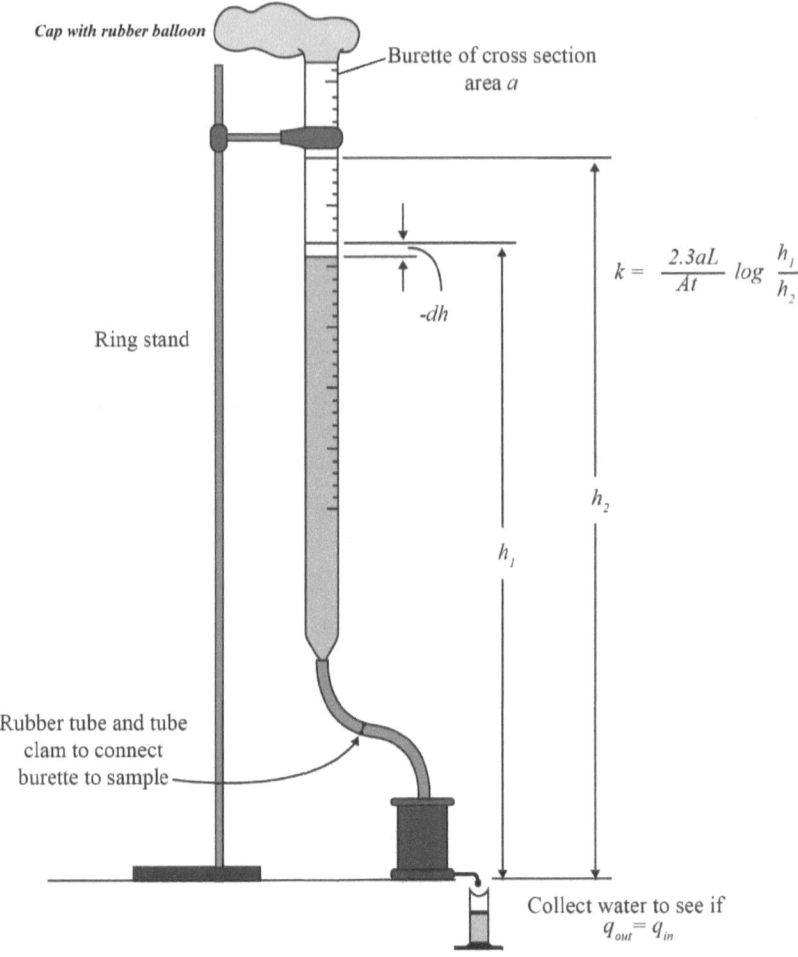

Cap with rubber balloon

Burette of cross section area a

$$k = \frac{2.3aL}{At} \, log \, \frac{h_1}{h_2}$$

$-dh$

Ring stand

h_2

h_1

Rubber tube and tube clam to connect burette to sample

Collect water to see if $q_{out} = q_{in}$

Figure 20. Schematic of the falling-head permeability setup

Apparatus:

○ Sample tube
○ Permeability device
○ Vessel containing de-aired water
○ Timer
○ Thermometer
○ Moisture content cans
○ Steel Wool

Preparation of Sample:

o Extrude the undisturbed sample carefully to inside the permeameter mould.
o Remove all disturbed material or material containing drilling mud from top and bottom of the sample

Testing Procedure:

o Measure and record the dimension and weight of the sample
o Place filter paper at both ends of the sample in the mould, clean rims and with gasket in place firmly secure the mould in the permeameter.
o Place the permeameter in a soaking tank in which the distilled water is about 5 cm above the tube top. Allow distilled water

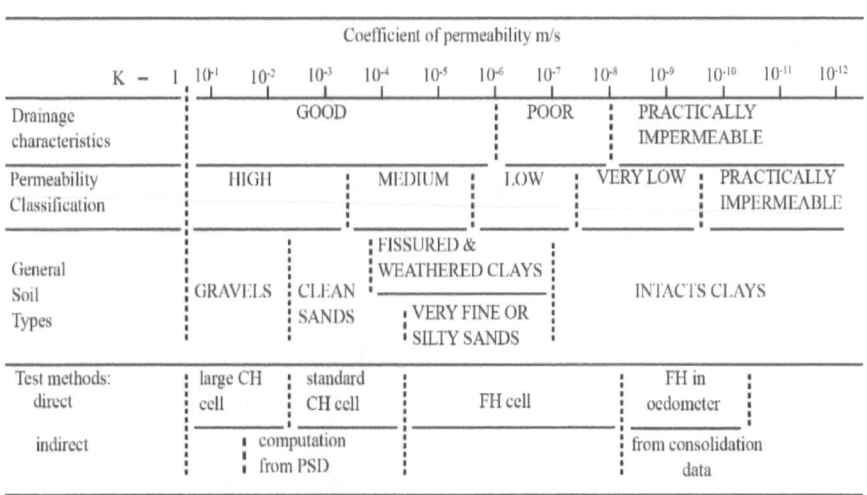

CH - constant head
FH - falling head
PSD - particle size distribution analysis

***Figure 21 Permeability and drainage
characteristics of main soil types***

to enter through bottom inlet of the tube and at the same time connect the upper tubing to a vacuum line to apply a small vacuum of the order of 5-8 cm Hg.

o   After ensuring that all air have been drawn out from the sample, clamp base tube and remove sample out of the tank to attach to the Falling Head Stand pipe.

o   Deair the lines by opening the hose clamp on the base and allow water to come out from the top.

o   Fill the burette to a convenient height and measure the hydraulic head across the sample and record it as h_1.

o   Open the exit tube and start the stop watch. Allow some water to flow through the sample and take a hydraulic head reading and record as h_2 at an elapsed time of (t). Take the temperature $(T \degree c)$ of the test.

o   Repeat operations (VI and VII) 2-3 times.

Calculations:

Calculate the coefficient of permeability as:

$$k = 0.023x \; \frac{aL}{AT} \log_{10} \left(\frac{h_1}{h_2}\right) R_T$$

(34)

Where

k	=	coefficient of permeability, m/sec
a	=	x-sectional area of manometer tube, sq. cm
L	=	length of sample, cm
A	=	x-sectional area of sample, sq. cm
t	=	$t_1 - t_2$ elapsed time, sec
h_1	=	initial head of water (at time t_1), cm
h_2	=	final head of water (at time t_2), sec
R_T	=	temperature correction or viscosity correction from Table10, (Bowles, 1970)

Table 10. Viscosity Corrections for η_T / η_{20}

^0_c	0	0.1	0.2	0.3	0.4	0.4	0.5	0.6	0.7	0.8
10	1.3012	1.2976	1.2940	1.2903	1.2867	1.2831	1.2795	1.2759	1.2122	1.2686
11	1.2650	1.2615	1.2580	1.2545	1.2510	1.2476	1.2441	1.2406	1.2871	1.2336
12	1.2301	1.2268	1.2234	1.2201	1.2168	1.2135	1.2101	1.2068	1.2035	1.2001
13	1.1968	1.1936	1.1905	1.1873	1.1841	1.1810	1.1777	1.1746	1.1714	1.1583
14	1.1651	1.1621	1.1590	1.1560	1.1529	1.1499	1.1469	1.1438	1.1408	1.1377
15	1.1347	1.1318	1.1289	1.1260	1.1231	1.1202	1.1172	1.1143	1.1114	1.1085
16	1.1056	1.1028	1.0999	1.0971	1.0943	1.0915	1.0887	1.0859	1.0803	1.0802
17	1.0774	1.0747	1.0720	1.0693	1.0667	1.0640	1.0613	1.0586	1.0560	1.0533
18	1.0507	1.0480	1.0454	1.0429	1.0403	1.0377	1.0351	1.0325	1.0300	1.0274
19	1.0248	1.0223	1.0198	1.0174	1.0149	1.0124	1.0099	1.0074	1.0050	1.0025
20	1.0000	0.9976	0.9952	0.9928	0.9904	0.9881	0.9857	0.9833	0.9809	0.9785
21	0.9761	0.9738	0.9715	0.9692	0.9669	0.9646	0.9623	0.9600	0.9577	0.9554
22	0.9531	0.9509	0.9487	0.9465	0.9443	0.9421	0.9399	0.9377	0.9355	0.9333
23	0.9311	0.9290	0.9268	0.9247	0.9225	0.9204	0.9183	0.9161	0.9140	0.9118
24	0.9097	0.9077	0.9056	0.9036	0.9015	0.8995	0.8975	0.8954	0.8934	0.9813
25	0.8893	0.8873	0.8853	0.8833	0.8813	0.8794	0.8774	0.8754	0.8734	0.8714
26	0.8694	0.8675	0.8655	0.8636	0.8617	0.8598	0.8579	0.8560	0.8540	0.8521
27	0.8502	0.8484	0.8465	0.8447	0.8428	0.8410	0.8392	0.8373	0.8355	0.8336
28	0.8318	0.8300	0.8282	0.8264	0.8246	0.8229	0.8211	0.8193	0.8175	0.8157
29	0.8139	0.8122	0.8105	0.8087	0.8070	0.8053	0.8036	0.8019	0.8001	0.7984
30	0.7967	0.7950	0.7934	0.7917	0.7901	0.7884	0.7867	0.7851	0.7834	0.7818
31	0.7801	0.7785	0.7769	0.7753	0.7737	0.7721	0.7705	0.7689	0.7673	0.7657
32	0.7641	0.7626	0.7610	0.7595	0.7579	0.7564	0.7548	0.7533	0.7517	0.7502
33	0.7486	0.7471	0.7456	0.7440	0.7425	0.7410	0.7395	0.7380	0.7364	0.7349
34	0.7334	0.7320	0.7305	0.7291	0.7276	0.7262	0.7247	0.7233	0.7218	0.7204
35	0.7189	0.7175	0.7161	0.7147	0.7133	0.7120	0.7106	0.7092	0.7078	0.7064

Reporting:

Report the coefficient of permeability in m/sec together with description of sample and its void ratio.

SOIL MECHANICS LABORATORY

DETERMINATION OF COEFFICIENT OF PERMEABILITY

Job No.:	Project:	Test Date:
Location:	Sample Description:	
Boring No.:	Specimen: D = cm; L = cm; A = cm^2	
Sample No.:	Tested By:	
Depth, m:	Supervisor:	

CONSTANT HEAD PERMEABILITY TEST DATA

TEST NO.	ELAPSED TIME t, Sec.	Q, cc	HEAD, h, Cm.	T^o C	k_T, m/Sec.	η_T/η_{20}	k_{20}, m/Sec.
Average							

FALLING HEAD PERMEABILITY TEST DATA

TEST NO.	ELAPSED TIME, t, Sec.	BURETTE a, cm^2	h_1, cm	h_2, cm	T^oC	k_T, m/Sec.	η_T/η_{20}	k_{20}, m/Sec.

Formulas:

1. Const. Head $k_T = \dfrac{QL}{hAt} \times 10^{-2}$ (m/sec)

2. Falling Head $k_T = \dfrac{aL}{At}$ In. $\dfrac{h_1}{h_2} \times 10^{-2}$ (m/sec)

3. $k_{20} = k_T \times \eta_T/\eta_{20}$ (m/sec)

Remarks:

6. SOIL CHEMICAL TESTS

Soil chemical testing program for civil engineering purposes is usually limited. It includes only those selected constituents whose presence is very important in majority of civil engineering works, particularly in conjunction with foundation engineering.

6.1 DETERMINATION OF SULPHATE CONTENT OF SOILS

Determination of Sulphate Content of soil is important since Sulphate attacks concrete. Water soluble sulphates are much more aggressive to concrete. Most usually found water soluble sulphates are Sodium Sulphate ($NaSO_4$) and Magnesium Sulphate ($MgSO_4$).

Scope:

This test outlines the procedure for determining water soluble sulphate content of soil using Gravimetrical method in which sulphates are precipitated as insoluble Barium Sulphate.

The method involves:

○ Preparing an aqueous extract of the soil
○ Treating with $BaCl_2$
○ Filtering off the resulting BaSO precipitation and weighing it

Apparatus and reagents:

Apparatus:

○ Bottle shaker, 300 ml capacity, with rubber bung
○ Electric muffle furnace
○ Balance: accuracy 0.001 gm

- Porcelain crucibles 40 mm in diameter
- Miscellaneous: 500 ml. beaker, Whitman Nos. 44 & 50 filter paper, glass rod, funnel etc.

Reagents are:

- Barium chloride, 5%solution (Dissolve 50 gm of Barium chloride in 1 litre of distilled water).
  CAUTION: NOTE THAT BARIUM CHLORIDE IS POISONOUS.
- Concentrated Hydrochloride acid (SG: 1.18)
- Indicators: Methyl red indicator (preferable) or blue litmus paper
- Silver nitrate, 5% solution
- ALL REAGENTS SHALL BE OF ANALYTICAL REAGENT GRADE

Specimen preparation:

- Grind the sample to powder form and quarter it
- Take representative oven dried sample of the mass of 10 gm on to a watch-glass

Test procedure:

- Take and record the mass of sample accurately to the nearest 0.001 gm. Transfer the soil mass to the shaking bottle, add 150 ml of distilled water and cap with rubber bung.
- Place the bottle in the shaker and shake for 30 minutes.
- Filter the soil suspension through a Whitman 50 filter paper and collect the filtrate in a 500 ml beaker. Wash the soil in the filter paper with a further 50 ml of distilled water.
- Add two drops of methyl red indicator solution to the filtrate and then add a few drops of HC1 to acidify it (red coloration) and then heat to boiling point using Bunsen flame.

- ○ Add $BaCl_2$ solution slowly (drop by drop) to the hot liquid while stirring it until no further precipitation is obtained.
- ○ Filter the precipitate on Whitman No. 44 filter paper and wash with hot distilled water until the washings are free from chloride. CHECK A DROP OF FILTRATE WITH LITTLE SILVER NITRATE SOLUTION, NO TURBIDITY IS AN INDICATION OF NO PRESENCE OF CHLORIDE.
- ○ Transfer the filter paper and residue to a porcelain crucible which has previously been ignited and weighed to 0.001 gm. Place the crucible and contents in an electrical muffle furnace at room temperature and then raise the temperature slowly to red heat (800°C) and maintain for 60 minutes. DO NOT ALLOW FILTER PAPER TO INFLAME - IT SHOULD CHAR SLOWLY. Remove the crucible to a desiccator and when cooled, weigh accurately to the nearest 0.001 gm and record it.

Calculations:.

The sulphate content, SO_3 is calculated as

$$SO_3 (\%) = \frac{34.3 \times W_2}{W_1} \tag{35}$$

where

W_1 = weight of oven dried soil, mgm
W_2 = weight of $BaSO_4$ precipitate mgm.

Reporting:

Report Sulphate (SO_3) content in a soil to the nearest 0.01%, by weight of original oven-dried soil.

6.2 DETERMINATION OF CHLORIDE CONTENT OF SOIL

This test is important because aqueous solutions of chloride cause corrosion of iron and steel when used as reinforcement cement in concrete.

Scope:

This test covers the determination of water soluble chloride content as equivalent Sodium Chloride salt content in the soil using Mohr's method.

The test involves:

i.   Preparation of test solution and a blank.
ii. Titration with 0.01N or 0.02N Silver Nitrate solution using Potassium Chromate as an indicator.

NOTES: THE TEST MAY BE PROCEEDED BY THE FOLLOWING QUICK QUALITATIVE TEST WHICH IS QUITE USEFUL TO INDICATE THE PRESENCE OF CHLORIDE IN THE SOIL.

○   TAKE 5 ML OF A 1:1 SOIL WATER EXTRACT IN A TEST TUBE
○   ACIDIFY IT, IF NECESSARY, BY ADDING A FEW DROPS OF NITRIC ACID
○   ADD A FEW DROPS OF 1% SILVER NITRATE SOLUTION AND OBSERVE THE TURBIDITY.
○   "AN APPRECIABLE TURBIDITY IS INDICATIVE OF THE PRESENCE OF CHLORIDE IN A MEASURABLE QUANTITITY."

Apparatus and Reagents:.

○   Balance: Accuracy 0.1 gm
○   Conical Flask: Capacity 250 ml
○   Burette (capacity: 50 ml) with stand
○   Glass bottles (capacity 500 ml) with stopper
○   Drying oven: Thermostatically controlled at 110± 5°C
○   Miscellaneous:
    -   Whatman Filter paper Nos.541 and 4Ash less tablets
    -   Filtration funnel

- Sulphuric acid: 0.01N solution
- Silver Nitrate: 0.02 or 0.01N solution
- Potassium chromate saturated solution
- Indicator paper (pH 6.0 - 7.0)

Preparation of sample and chemical solution:

Sample

- Mix the sample thoroughly and divide it by quartering or by riffling.
- Take about 1 kg of soil containing particles less than 20 mm. Oven dry the sample at 110±5°C and after allowing to cool down, crush the particles to pass through 600μm sieve (No. 30 sieve).
- Dry again the crushed material in the oven and allow cooling in the desiccator. Take about 100 gm of soil and place it in a 500 ml bottle.

Solution

- Add 200 ml of distilled water to the soil sample which is already taken in the 500 ml bottle. Replace the stopper and shake frequently for 24 hours. DO NOT APPLY HEAT.
- Filter a portion of the extract, if necessary, and take 25 ml by means of a pipette in a 250 ml conical flask to acidify with 0.02N Sulphuric acid. IF THE CONCENTRATION OF CHLORIDE IS HIGH, TAKE 5-10 ML EXTRACT ONLY AND DILUTE IT WITH DISTILLED WATER TO MAKE UP 25 ML SOLUTION.
- Add two drops of saturated Potassium chromate solution.
- Prepare two blank solutions in the following manner:
  Take two similar conical flasks each containing 25 ml distilled water and also add to them the same quantity of saturated Potassium chromate solution. These are used for color comparison and blank determination.

Test procedure:

○ Titrate the blank with 0.02N Silver Nitrate solution until a permanent blood red tinge is just obtained and remain permanent.
○ Titrate the test solution in the same way and record the volume of Silver Nitrate solution.
IF THE CHLORIDE CONTENT IS VERY HIGH, USE 0.1 SOLUTION OF SILVER NITRATE IN BOTH THE TEST AND BLANK SOLUTIONS.

Calculation:

Calculate the content of soluble Chloride (Cl) as the equivalent Sodium Chloride content from the equations:

(a) For 0.02 N Silver Nitrate solution (Chloride content high)

$$Cl\ (ppm) = \frac{25}{x} \cdot (1.17) \cdot \frac{V}{m} \cdot 10^6 \qquad (36)$$

(b) For 0.01 N Silver Nitrate solution (Chloride content low)

$$Cl\ (ppm) = \frac{25}{x} \cdot 5.85 \cdot \frac{V}{m} \cdot 10^6 \qquad (37)$$

Where:

x - volume of the extract, ml

v - volume of silver nitrate solution, ml

m - mass of dry soil, gm

Reporting:

Report the result as parts per million (ppm) to absolute figures.

6.3 DETERMINATION OF CARBONATE CONTENT OF SOIL

Carbonates in soil mainly occur as Calcium Carbonate or chalk. Generally chalky subgrades are susceptible to frost action. Chalky cohesive soils are noticed as more friable. Content of carbonate can be used as an index to assess the quality of chalk. As a foundation material, high content of carbonate means a low clay mineral content, and usually indicates a high strength. In cemented soils, the carbonate content, indicate the degree of cementation.

Scope:

This test covers the determination of the content of Calcium Carbonate (referred to as content of carbonate) in a soil using Collins method.

The test method involves:

o   Treating a weighed amount of soil with hydrochloric acid.
o   Measuring the volume of carbon-dioxide given off by the process.
o   Corrections for temperature and atmospheric pressure are applied.

Apparatus:

o   Drying oven: Thermostatically controlled at $110 \pm 5°C$
o   Balance: Accuracy 0.001 gm
o   Collins apparatus: see Fig. 22, *(Head, 1980).*
    -   Conical flask (B)
    -   Outlet (C)
    -   Hand pressure bulb (D)
    -   Graduated burette (E)
    -   Leveling tube (F)
    -   Tap (G)
    -   Two way tap (H) see Fig. 23 *(Head, 1980).*
    -   Reservoir flask (R)

- Perspex glass tank (T)
- Measuring cylinder (A) for hydrochloric acid

Reagent:

○ Hydrochloric acid solution (cemented HCl /Distilled water: 1/3).

Preparation of sample:

○ Break oven dry soil to pass US No. 4 sieve
○ Take a representative sample, by riffling, of the mass of 50 gm
○ Oven dry the sample and then allow for cooling in a desiccator.

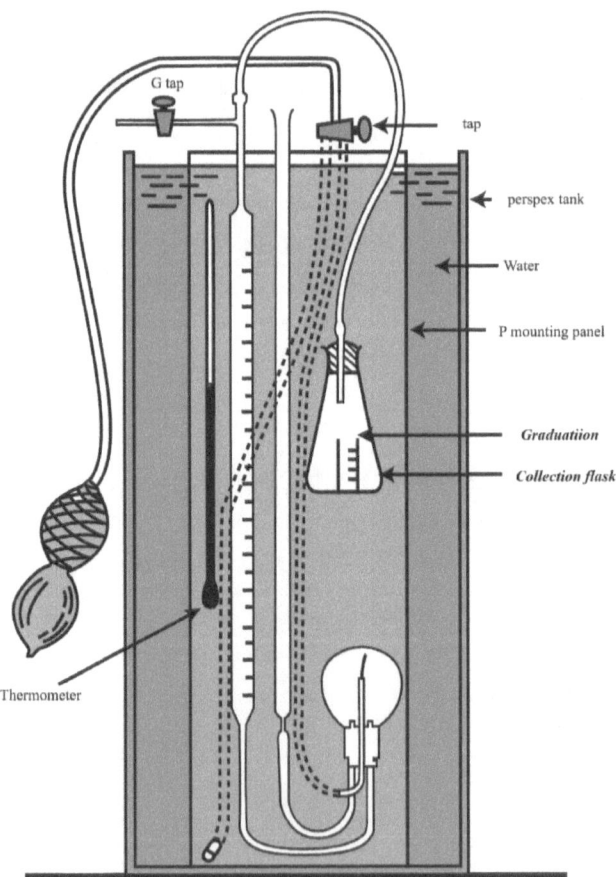

Figure 22. Diagrammatic arrangement of Collins Calcimeter

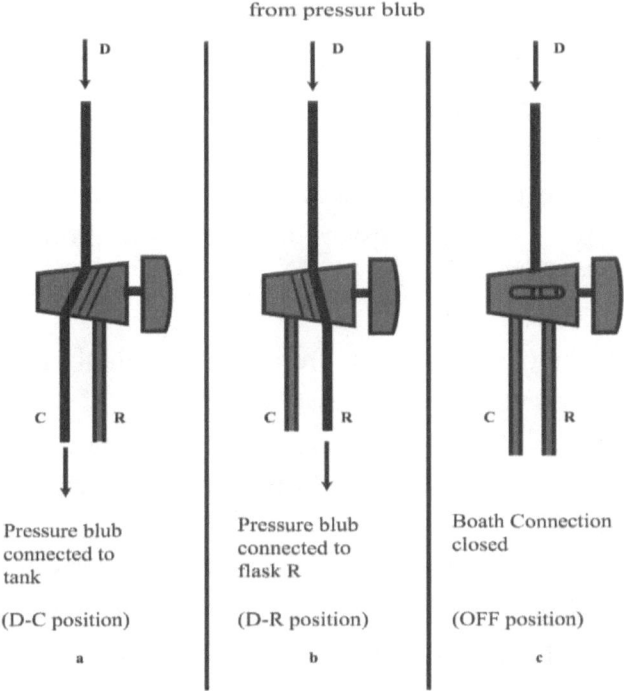

Figure 23. Two-way tap on Collins Calcimeter

Test Procedure:

○ Determine by trial the amount of sample required to evolve about 10-25 ml of CO_2 gas.

○ Weigh the oven dried sample accurate to 0.001 gm (W_1) and transfer them in the conical flask (B).

○ Fill glass tank (T) with water at room temperature to within 25 mm from the top. Pour water into the leveling tube (F) using funnel to half fill the reservoir with water.

○ Take 10-15 ml (V_a) of Hydrochloric acid (HCL) in graduated cylinder (A) and place it carefully in the flask (B). NO SPILLING OF THE ACID CAN BE ALLOWED FOR.

○ Connect the flask to the Collins apparatus using a rubber bung at the end of the tube and place it in the water tank and secure it into position.

○ Stir the water in the tank by closing the right hand vertical tap (D-C CONNECTION) and blowing air from the pressure bulb to obtain a uniform temperature $T^0{}_1 C$.

○ Open tap Gl set tap H to D-R connection. Bring water level in the burette E to zero mark by gentle pressure to the bulb thus automatically rising the water in adjoining tube F to the same level.

○ Close tap H. Release pressure to the bulb to drop water in the tube F. NOTE THAT LEVEL IN MEASURING TUBE E WILL ALSO SINK.

○ Remove the conical flask B from the water tank, tilt and shake and replace in the tank.

○ Set tap H to D-C connection, agitate the water with air from the pressure bulb until a uniform steady temperature TO C is established.

○ Set tap H to D-R position squeeze gently the pressure bulb until the water level in both tubes E and F are equal. Close tap H (OFF POSITION) and record the volume indicated in the burette E.

Repeat the process of removing the flask B, shaking and returning to the water tank and adjusting the level in tubes E and F until there is no further increase in volume of gas evolved is observed by burette E. Record the final reading as the volume of CO_2 gas evolved (V_g ml) If the temperature $T_2{}^\circ C$ differs $T_1{}^\circ C$, subtract 0.1ml from the increase in the gas volume for every ($0.2^\circ C$) rise in temperature and vice versa.

○ Record the barometric pressure at the time of test.

Calculation:

The carbonate content (expressed as CO_2) of the sample can be calculated using the following equation:

$$\text{Carbonate (as } CO_2) = \frac{W_2 \times V_g}{1000W_1} \qquad (38)$$

Where:

W_1 = Dry mass of soil gm
W_2 = Mass gm of 100 ml of CO_2
V_g = Volume of acid, ml
V_a = Volume of CO_2 gas evolved, ml

Report:

Report the results and the percentage of C_3O_3 (to two significant figures.

Table 11. Data for Collins Calcimeter Test (after Head, 1980)

T_m (°C)	Mass W_2 (uncorrected) Volume of acid used, V_a (ml)								Corrections for pressure Barometric pressure (mm Hg)					Corrections for volume V_g (ml)			
	10	12	14	16	18	20	30	40	740	750	760	770	780	0-9	10-19	20-29	30-40
12	198	201	204	208	211	214	230	240	-6	-3	0	+3	+6	+1	0	0	-1
14	196	199	202	204	207	210	226	244	-5	-3	0	+3	+5	+1	0	0	-1
16	193	196	198	201	203	206	221	238	-5	-3	0	+3	+5	+2	0	0	-2
18	191	193	196	198	201	203	216	233	-5	-3	0	+3	+5	+2	+1	-1	-2
20	188	190	193	195	198	200	212	228	-5	-3	0	+3	+5	+3	+1	-1	-3
22	186	188	190	192	194	196	208	223	-5	-3	0	+3	+5	+3	+1	-1	-3
24	183	185	187	189	191	193	204	218	-5	-3	0	+3	+5	+5	+3	-3	-5
26	181	183	185	186	188	190	200	213	-5	-3	0	+3	+5	+8	+4	-4	-8
28	178	180	182	183	185	187	196	208	-5	-3	0	+3	+5				
30	176	178	179	181	182	184	192	203				+3	+5				

Notes:
1. Data are void for a 150 ml raction flask (B)
2. The main section of the table gives the mass of 100 ml CO_2 (mg) based upon a measured volume of CO_2 at 760 mm Hg pressure, and at mean temperatures between 12 and 30°C (T_m).
3. The correction sections show values to be added or subtracted for different pressures and measured volumes of CO_2.

Example: V_a = 20 ml, T_m = 22°C, barometer reading 750 mm Hg, V_g = 10 ml. Therefore ml of CO_2 weighs: 196 -3 + 1 = 194 mg = W_2.

If the dry mass of sample used was 2.51 g = W_1, carbonate content % (as CO_2) = $\frac{194 \times 10}{1000 \times 2.51}$ = 0.77%

* Based on data supplied by Macfarlane Robson Ltd., Blaydon-on-Tyne, Durham, manufacturers of the Collins' Calcimeter and slide-rule.

BIBLIOGRAPHY

Akroyd, T.N.W. 91969), *"Laboratory Testing in Soil Engineering",* Soil Mechanics Ltd. London.

American Society for Testing Materials abbreviated as ASTM (1982) *Annual Book of ASTM Standards",* Parts 14 & 19.

Bowles, J.E. (1970), *Engineering Properties of Soils and their Measurement"* McGraw-Hill Book Co.

Head, K.H. (1980), *"Manual of Soil Laboratory"* Vols. 1 entitled Soil Classification and Compaction Tests, Pentech Press, London.

Head, K.H. (1982), *"Manual of Soil Laboratory Testing"* Vol. 2 entitled Permeability, Shear Strength and Compressibility Tests, John Wiley and Sons.

Lambe T.W. (1967), *"Soil Testing for Engineers"* John Wiley and Sons, Inc.

Saeedy, H. (1980), *"Soil Engineering and its Applications",* University of Basra Press, Basra, Iraq.

Stokes, Sir George G. (1891), *Mathematical and Physical Paper III",* Cambridge University Press.

Teng, W.C. (1962), *"Foundation Design",* Prentice-Hall International, Inc., New Jersey

Thornton, S.I. and Welch. R.C. (1975), *Arkansas Bridge Foundations: Laboratory Testing"* Interim Report, Arkansas Highway and Transportation Department Arizona.

Transport and Road Research Laboratory abbreviated as TRRL (1974), *Soil Mechanics for Road Engineers",* HMSO, London.

Welch, R.C. and Thornton, S.I. (1977), "Arkansas *Bridge Foundations: Laboratory Investigations"* Interim Report, Arkansas Highway and Transportation Department Arizona.

PART II

GEOTECHNICAL - GEOHYDROLOGICAL FIELD MANUAL

PREFACE

This manual has been prepared mainly as a guide and aid for the practicing engineers and professionals to help in their planning and supervision of field works. It contains technical information on geotechnical field investigation comprising of field testing, sampling and description of soil samples. The contents have been extended to suit some applications and requirements for geohydrological needs, to include the followings:

1. Installation of Standpipe piezometer.
2. Field permeability tests.
3. Pressuremeter testing.

The manual contains both detailed standardized procedures that have been found useful for obtaining uniform results and also general guide lines intended to assist but not substitute for engineering judgment

Theoretical aspects have been deliberately minimized on the understanding that they are covered in text books.

As a whole, attempts were made to make the manual brief and concise, yet readable and understandable by civil engineers with no or little geotechnical background.

1. INTRODUCTION

This manual was basically developed to include and not limited to the study, design and construction supervision of a pilot drainage project involving an extensive geotechnical investigation.

The field works are comprised of drilling boreholes and water wells, field testing and sampling of soils and water for laboratory testing. Initially, the investigation was to cover various sites.

Out of these, two selected sites were to undergo further detailed investigations.

The field tests include:

1. Standard Penetration Tests (SPT).
2. Installation of Piezometers.
3. Field permeability testing in bore holes and pumping test in wells.

Samples for geotechnical laboratory testing will be taken from small diameter (100mm) boreholes while cores for soil profile shall be taken from large diameter holes.

The work was executed through contractors specialized in the field under the supervision of qualified professionals for which they were prepared. It is intended to acquaint them with work before they go to field. Test procedures and guidelines are given to help execution of the field work according to the most internationally recognized specifications

1.1   Responsibilities and duties of Geotechnical field staff.

The geotechnical field staff must recognize the significance of geotechnical field investigations.

As in the case with all geotechnical studies, those not involving field investigations and those that fail to produce a credible data base or credible field test results could be useless, no matter how sophisticated the laboratory equipment or the methods computation used in geotechnical evaluations.

Engineering supervision is the key to ensuring the quality of field work. The geotechnical field staff must therefore be familiar with the purpose of the investigation and the investigation techniques.

The geotechnical field staff will be responsible for the engineering supervision of the geotechnical field investigation and will have the following specific responsibilities.

1. Supervise the acquisition and field study of the disturbed soil samples, cores and prepare geotechnical logs.
2. Supervise the acquisition of the undisturbed soil samples.
3. Identify sampling and coring intervals.
4. Provide necessary assistance to the Field Coordinator in supervising the drilling contractor and in ensuring that the technical specifications for geotechnical sampling and testing are met.
5. Supervise geotechnical field testing and record test results.
6. Place the disturbed and undisturbed samples and cores in appropriate containers clearly marked with the well No. and the designated laboratory.
7. Observe the safety regulations and instructions at the drilling site.

2. STANDARD PENETRATION TEST

2.1   Standard Penetration Test (SPT)

This test measures the resistance to the penetration of a standard sampler. The test was originally developed in 1927 by Raymond Pile Co. but owes its popularity to Terzaghi and Peck (1948). Extensive studies, leading to development of correlations for foundation, made it a most popular soil test and is now used all over the world.

SPT tests will be carried out according to the specifications of Standard Method ASTM D 1586 (1967, Reapproved 1974) and as directed by the supervising geotechnical engineer.

2.2   Definition

Standard penetration resistance (or 'N' value) is defined as the number of blows required to drive a split-spoon sampler with a 30-inch (76 cm) free fall of a standard hammer weighing 140 lbf. (63.5 kgf.), a distance of 12 in (30 cm) after an initial penetration of 6 in (15 cm). When full penetration of spoon is not possible, the number of below together the fractional penetration shall be mentioned.

2.3   Equipment

Acker Drill Co., 1974 developed the equipment required for conducting SPT tests shall include the following (Fig. 1):

*   Drilling equipment capable of providing a clean borehole and driving the sampler.
*   Split-spoon sampler.
*   Complete SPT device, as defined.

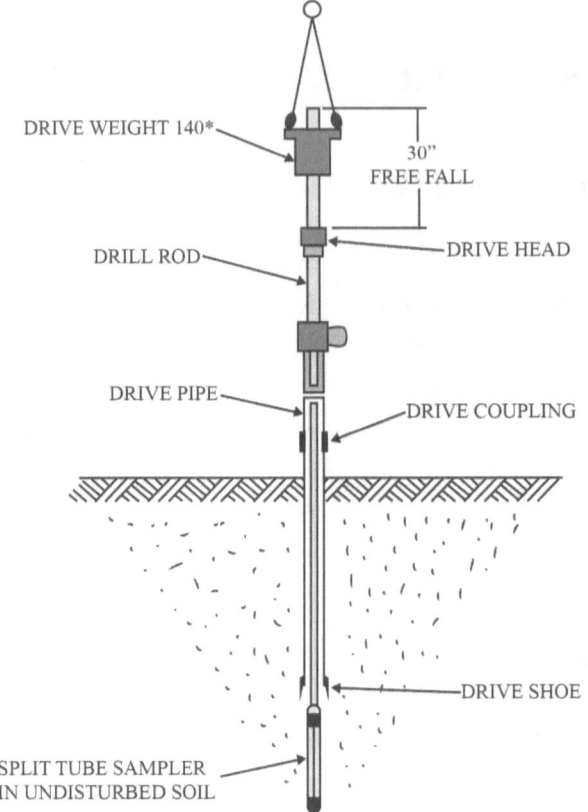

Figure 1. Equipment required for the standard penetration test.

2.4   Borehole Diameter

For geotechnical investigations, the borehole should be limited in diameter to between 2 1/4 and 6" (57.2 and 152 mm).

2.5   Frequency of Testing

It is standard practice to perform the test at every 1.0 or 1.5 m or at each change of stratification down to a 10-m depth. Below this depth, the testing interval will be specified on site by the supervision geotechnical engineer to ensure proper and meaningful information about the soil strata in question.

2.6   *Procedure (ASTM D1586-67, Reapproved 1974)*

1. Stop advancement of the borehole at the depth at which the SPT Test will be conducted and the disturbed soil sample will be collected.

2. Clean the borehole of all loose or disturbed soil, segregated coarse material, and any clay adhering to the walls. When casing is used, the cleaning shall extend to at least the bottom edge of the casing and the borehole shall be advanced a few centimeters further to bypass the disturbances caused by the cutting edge of the casing. Cleaning shall be done with deflected jets, shielded jets or suitable cleanout augers, for boreholes advanced using water. For holes advanced using mud and tricone bit, cleaning may be done by circulating mud through the tricone bit. No bottom-discharge bits are permitted, but side-discharge bits would be acceptable.

3. Clean and lubricate thoroughly the inside of the sampler.

4. Lower the sample down the borehole ensuring that it reaches that exact sampling depth drilled and is seated in undisturbed soil. Maintain the borehole full of water when sampling below the water table. This measure will be adopted to ensure hydraulic balance at the test elevation.

5. With driving assembly on top of drill rods, advance the sampling spoon by driving until 18" (45 cm) have been penetrated or until - 100 blows - have been struck. Sampling in non-cohesive soil may require the insertion of a retainer between the cutting shoe and the sampling barrel.

6. Count and record the number of blows required to drive each 15 cm of penetration or part of it. The number of blows for the last 30 cm penetration shall be recorded as "N" value.

7. Turn the drill rod to shear the end of the sampler. Take the sampler out of the borehole slowly by jacking it against the hydraulic drill and open it to collect the sample *(Joyce, 1982) as* in (Figure 2).

8. Give proper labels for identification purpose (Section 4.3).

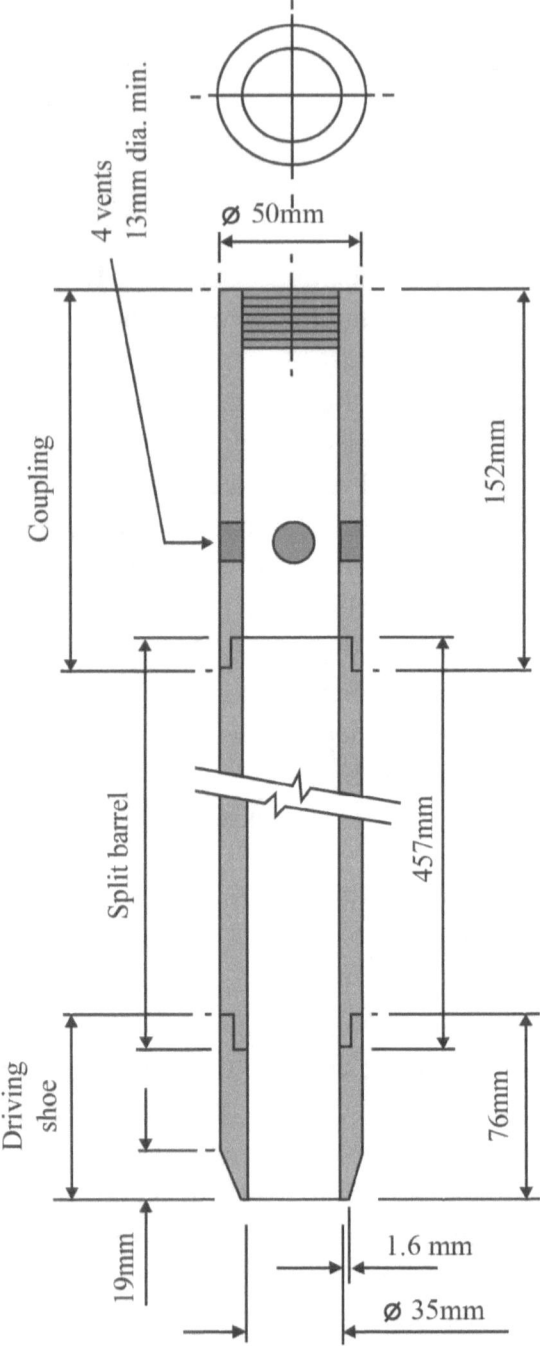

Figure 2. Split spoon sampler.

2.7   Possible Sources of Error in SPT Soundings

2.7.1   Drilling:

- Inadequate cleaning of the hole prior to the SPT count.
- Improper seating of sampler in disturbed material.
- Spoon driving in the soil above the bottom of the casing
- Inadequate hydrostatic head in the hole.
- Sampler plugged by gravel or cemented aggregations.
- Overdriving the sampler.
- Overwashing ahead of casing.

2.7.2.   Drive Assembly:

- Non-standard hammer or drop
- Not attaining the correct free fall or non-free fall of the drive weight.
- Eccentric drive cap or failure to use a guide rod.
- Eccentric.

2.7.3   Sampler: Rusted or damaged split spoon tip

2.7.4   Recording:

Inaccurate recording of the blow counts and penetration

2.7.5   Human Error:

Last but not least, operator's error.

3. SAMPLING

3.1   Collection of Disturbed Soil Samples

The disturbed soil samples will be collected with a split-spoon sampler, the way the SPT is carried out. The disturbed soil samples are to be used for physical and soil classification tests.

3.2   Equipment

* Split-spoon sampler.
    ID 1 3/8 inch or 35 mm.
    OD 2 inch or 50 mm.
    Minimum length 18 inches, or 450 mm.
* Shoe: Sharp-cutting edge
* Valve: Reliable check valve at the top.

3.3   Sampling Interval

Same as the SPT interval (see Section 2.5).

3.4   Procedure

Follow steps 1 through 8 in Section 2.6 on SPT testing.

3.5   Collection of Undisturbed Soil Samples

Undisturbed soil samples are used in laboratory determinations of engineering properties, i.e., strength and compressibility characteristics.

3.6   Sampling Frequency

Sampling frequency will be as specified in the technical specifications unless instructed otherwise by the Supervising Engineer.

3.7   Sampler Description

Undisturbed samples will be collected using the thin-wall tube sampler, also known as the Shelby tube. This is only applicable for soft formations. For dense cohesionless soil, use a Denison/Pitcher sampler of appropriate dimension provided the proper undisturbed samples are obtainable.

3.7.1   Thin-wall Tube Sampler

The thin-wall tube sampler is shown in Fig. 3. It consists of cold drawn steel tubing and may be of variable length. The sampler head has vents for the escape of drill mud and also equipped with a ball check valve to prevent entrance of drill mud during withdrawal and to assist in creating a vacuum above the soil which aids in retaining the soil core.

Sampling Procedure

1. Stop the borehole at the appropriate sampling depth.
2. Clean the borehole or casing with a deflected jet or cleanout auger or by circulating mud through a tricone bit.
3. Clean and lubricate thoroughly the inside of the sampling tube.
4. Push the sampler into the soil at a rate of 75 to 150 mm/s by hydraulic pressure or mechanical jacking. Record the pressure required. When the sampler has to be driven with a drop hammer, record the hammer weight, height of drop, and the number of blows for each 15 cm penetration, or part of it.

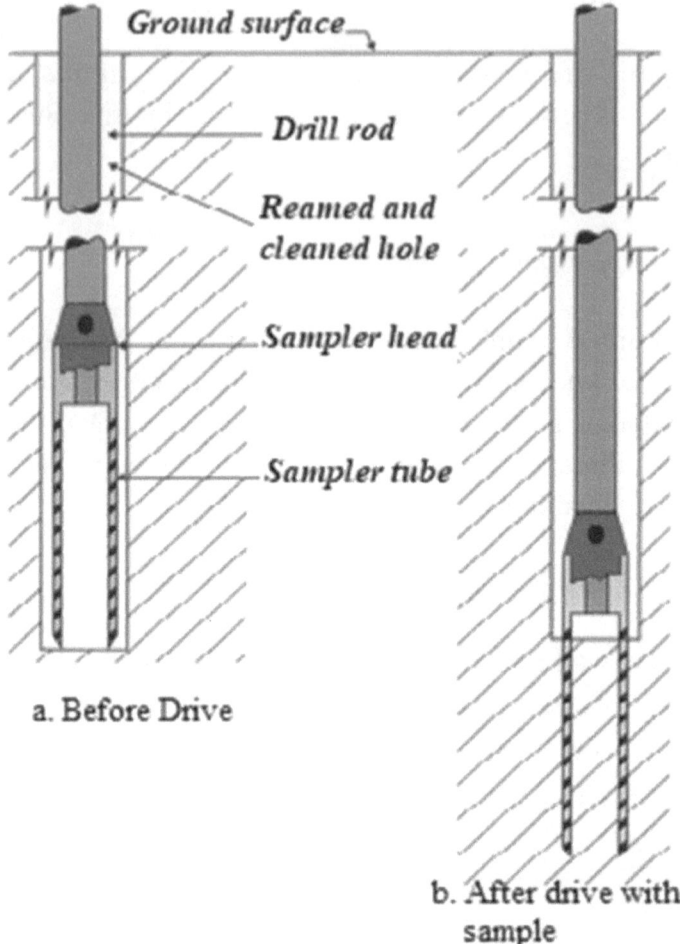

Ground surface

Drill rod

Reamed and
cleaned hole

Sampler head

Sampler tube

a. Before Drive

b. After drive with
sample

Figure 3. Sampling with thin wall table sampler.

5. Maintain the hole full of water when sampling below the water table. In saturated sands and silts, withdraw the drill bit slowly before inserting the sampler to prevent loosening of the soil around the hole.

6. Turn the drill rod to shear the end of the sampler. Take the sampler out of the hole slowly by jacking it against the hydraulic drill.

7. Give proper labels to the sample for identification purpose (Section 4.3).

3.7.2 Denison Corebarrel

AS shown in *(Fig. 4)*. It is a triple tube swivel type core barrel. The outer barrel is equipped with corebit made of tungsten materials having cutting teeth on the bottom and rotates. The inner barrel is the sampler and has a liner made of 28 gauge sheet metal rolled into a cylinder and shouldered at the seam. It is provided with a shoe with a sharp cutting edge threaded to it. The Denison core barrel uses a basket type spring core catcher.

Procedure

1. Lower the corebarrel containing the sampler within a meter of the bottom of the borehole. Start circulation of drilling fluid. This will remove excess cutting that may have settled to the bottom.

2. Lower the corebarrel to the bottom of the bore hole. Rotate the outer barrel, force the inner barrel with the sampler downward at uniform rate. As the inner barrel is advanced, the outer barrel cuts out the soil between the two barrels, the fluid washes out the cuttings between the two barrels, and the inner barrel cuts out a sample.

3. When the sample is cored to one and half inch to two inch (38 - 50mm) of the final desired depth, then the drilling fluid is shut off and the coring operation is completed. Shutting off the fluid will wedge the cuttings between the inner and outer barrel shoes which will cause the inner barrel to rotate with the outer barrel, thus shearing the sample from the parent material. In addition, compaction of the soil in the inner barrel shoe will form a plug and assist in sample recovery.

4. After completion of the drive, withdraw the core barrel from the hole, with extreme care being taken at all times to avoid sample disturbance.

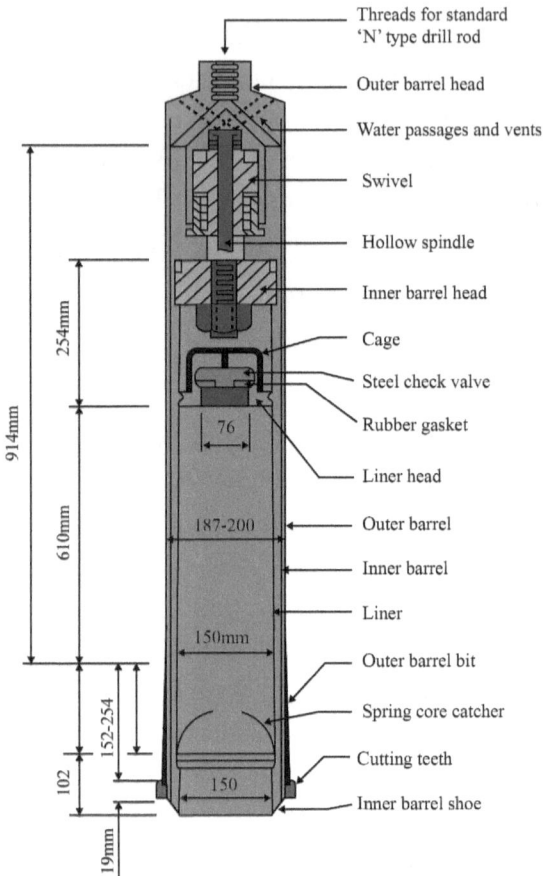

Figure 4. Denison Sampler

5. Remove the outer and inner barrel shoes without jarring the sample. Remove the liner tube with the soil core.

6. Remove the soil at both ends to a depth of 2 inches (50 mm) to a smooth flat surface. Place wooden filler block (previously waxed), inside the liner tube at each end and cover with melted wax. Crimp the tube over the wood fillers to hold them in place.

7. Collect soil retained in the inner barrel shoe and the soil removed from the top of the core for use for field inspection and classification.

8. Mark clearly the top and bottom of the sample, hole number, project feature and elevations or depths of sampling before shipment to the laboratory.

NOTES:

1. 1. (In step 2) the rate of penetration should not be greater than the speed at which the outer sampler is able to cut meaning that the downward force should be a minimum. Also the speed of rotation should be limited to that which will not tear or break the soil sample.
2. 2. Use the thinnest mud that produces satisfactory results.
3. 3. Pump pressure should be minimum amount necessary to circulate the mud freely and carry the cuttings from the hole. Too much drilling fluid pressure and flow will erode the core. On the other hand too little pressure and flow will allow the cuttings to enter the core barrel along with core and plug the bit. Experience is the best answer to properly regulate the bit pressure, speed of rotation and drill-fluid pressure.
4. 4. The total drive length should always be a few inches short of the length available for the sample to assure that the sample is not packed in the sampler.
5. 5. The core catcher should not be used unless it is absolutely necessary to retain the soil.

3.7.3   Pitcher Sampler

The pitcher sampler *(Earth manual, 1974)* in Fig. 5, like the Denison core barrel is a type of modified double tube core barrel sampler. The inner barrel consists of a thin walled sampler tube with a rolled and reamed cutting edge which is fixed to the inner tube head by set screws. The outer barrel has a diamond or tungsten insert core bit. The inner barrel is spring loaded and telescopes in and out of the cutter bit as the hardness of the material varies.

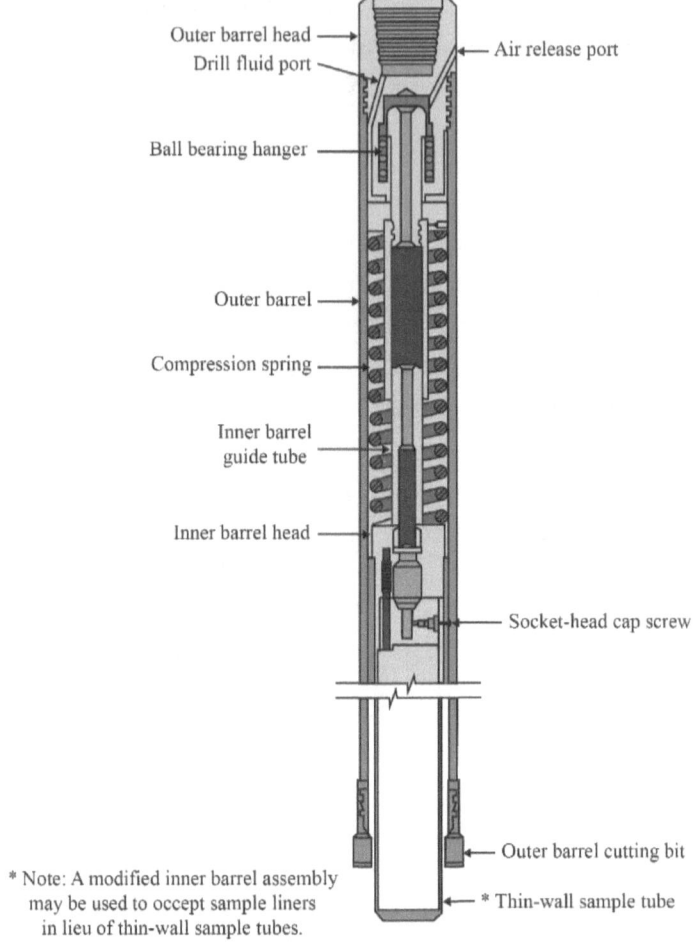

Outer barrel head

Drill fluid port

Air release port

Ball bearing hanger

Outer barrel

Compression spring

Inner barrel
guide tube

Inner barrel head

Socket-head cap screw

Outer barrel cutting bit

* Note: A modified inner barrel assembly
may be used to occept sample liners
in lieu of thin-wall sample tubes.

* Thin-wall sample tube

Figure 5. Pitcher sampler.

Procedure

The procedure for obtaining undisturbed samples with the pitcher sampler is the same as for the Denison corebarrel with the following exceptions.

1. It is not necessary to use different inner barrel shoes.
2. After the sampler has been withdrawn from the hole the thin wall-tube is removed and the sample maybe sealed in the tube using expanding packers or extruded preserved.

4. PRESERVATION AND TRANSPORTATION OF SAMPLES

4.1   Split-Spoon Samples/Drill Cuttings

Collect representative specimens of each sample as soon as they are taken to preserve the original moisture content. The containers for the preservation of samples shall be round, screw top, airtight, clean glass jars of at least 0.5 1 capacity. Samples so preserved shall be suitably boxed, marked and identified with legible labels. (See Section 4.3).

4.2   Undisturbed Samples

Remove a maximum of 25 mm of the undisturbed material from the top and bottom end of each sample from the sampling tube. Fill the ends of the sample tube to the top with paraffin added in succession (to prevent voids), then cap them with tight-fitting plastic caps. For porous samples place a layer of waxed paper over the exposed ends of the sample to protect them from contamination by the molten paraffin. Undisturbed samples and cores shall be labeled and identified giving special attention to marking the top and bottom. Exercise care when handling and shipping to minimize disturbance.

4.3   Sample Labels.

Sample labels shall be prepared in duplicate with one label included with the sample inside the sample container and the other on the outside.

The samples shall be labeled and boxed as follows:

4.3.1 Disturbed Samples

- Date
- Project Name
- Location
- BH No.
- Jar No.
- Sample No.
- Elevation of E.G.S (m MD)
- Depth of sample (m)
- Penetration ('N' value blows/each 75 mm):
- Name of Collector
- Remarks

NOTES:

1. E.G.S: Existing ground surface
2. MD: Municipality Datum

4.3.2 Undisturbed Samples

These samples shall have printed labels giving the following information:

- Project
- Location
- BH No
- Sample No
- Elevation of E.G.S. (m MD):
- Depth of sample (m)
- Length of sample (cm)
- Sampler type
- Penetration ('N' value blows/each 75 mm)
- Description of material
- Name of collector

- Remarks

4.3.3. *Transportation Boxes*

Each box of samples shall be identified with weatherproof and water proof labels or markings indicating the following:

- Date
- Project
- Location
- BH No.
- Sample No.
- Box No.

5. FIELD IDENTIFICATION AND DESCRIPTION OF SOIL SAMPLES

Identification and description of soils is essential in the field and is of special significance to the geotechnical investigation. General guidelines in these contexts are given in the following sections. But it should be borne in mind that all of the descriptive data are not always necessary. Engineering judgment should be applied to include the pertinent information, to avoid negative information and to eliminate repetition.

5.1   Textural guide

The following soil classification guide, which is the ASTM D 422 standard (1972), provides a suitable guide for soil classification according to grain size or texture.

Primary Grouping	Component	Size (mm)	U.S. Sieve
Coarse Grained:			
	* Boulder	> 300	12"
	* Cobble	75-300	3"-12"
	* Gravel		
	Coarse	19-75	3/4"-3"
	Fine	4.75-19.00	No. 4-3/4"
	* Sand		
	Coarse	2.00-4.75	No.10 to No.4
	Medium	0.425-2.00	No.40 to No.10
	Fine	0.075-0.425	No.200 to No.40
Fine Grained:			
	* Silt		
	* Clay		Passing No.200

5.2   *Identification*

In the field, the identification of soil shall involve visual and hand examination of the characteristics of the soil particles, in conjunction with simple manual tests (whenever necessary), to estimate the approximate proportion of the particle sizes in the following manner:

5.2.1   *Gravel vs. Sand:*

- Visual examination: The particles of both sizes are visible to the naked eye. Gravel is larger than the size of the lead in an ordinary pencil.

5.2.2   *Sand vs. Silt:*

- Visual examination: Only the particles of sand size are visible to the naked eye.
- Dispersion test: Disperse a spoonful of the sample in a glass of water and observe the time it takes to settle. Sand grains will settle in a matter of 1 min, silt will take 15 min to 1 hr.

5.2.3   *Silt vs. Clay:*

- Visual examination: Particles of both sizes are invisible to the naked eye.
- Dispersion test: Disperse a spoonful to the sample in a glass of water and observe the time it takes to settle. Silt will take 15 min to 1 hour, clay remains in suspension for several hours.
- Shaking Test: Mix a spoonfull of the sample with water to make a paste and place it in the palm of your hand. Start shaking with a horizontal abrupt motion and observe the top surface. A shining surface will indicate the predominance of silt particles.

- Rolling Test: Mix a soil sample with some water and try to roll it into a thin thread of 1/8' inch (3 mm) diameter. Only with clayey soils is such a roll possible.
- Dry Strength Test: Dry a small soil sample in the air and test for breaking strength. If it contains no clay particles, the sample will crumble readily into powder.

5.3 Description

The soil can be identified and described after its principal component (or predominantly occurring component) such as gravel, sand, silt, or clay. If the sample is not dominated by any one component, it can be described by the two leading components as follows:

Clayey   Sand

(Next to major component)   (Major component)

Minor components may be described according to the following standard by Burmister (1948):

Term	Range (%) by weight of total soil
with a trace of_____	0-10
with a little_____	10-20
with some_____	20-35
and_____	35-50

5.4 Color Description

- * Single major color: Brown, grey, black
- * Major color appears modified: Brownish Grey Secondary or Major color Modifying color

* Two distinct colors swirled in the soil: mottled grey and brown.

5.5 Moisture Content

* Dry   - completely dry soil.
* Damp   - with very little water.
* Moist   - with a slight amount of water.
* Wet   - with an appreciable amount of water.
* Saturated - fully saturated with the water of submerged soil.

5.6 Relative Density of Coarse Grained Soil

SPT 'N' Value (Blows/30 cm)	Relative Density (After Terzaghi and Peck, 1948)
0-4	Very loose
4-10	Loose
10-30	Medium dense
30-50	Dense
> 50	Very dense

5.7 Consistency of Fine Grained Soil

Description	SPT-N Value	Hand Manipulation (Terzaghi and Peck, 1948)
Very soft	< 2	easily penetrated 50 mm by fist
Soft	2-4	Easily penetrated50 mm by thumb
Medium stiff	4-8	penetrated by thumb with moderate effort

Stiff	8-15	readily indented by thumb but not penetrated
Very stiff	15-30	readily indented by thumb nail
Hard	> 30	indented with difficulty by thumb nail

5.8   Shape of Coarse Soil Particles

For details see (Fig. 6)
- Angular
- Subangular
- Subrounded
- Rounded
- Very rounded

Angular   Subangular   Subrounded   Rounded   Very Rounded

Figure 6. Grain shapes of sand and gravel.

5.9   Size Distribution of Coarse Material

* Fine to coarse sand   : Almost equal proportions
* Coarse sand   : Coarse sand predominates (>50%)
* Medium to coarse sand : Medium and coarse sand dominate more than 50%

5.10   Secondary Inclusion

* Foreign matter   : wood, rubble, shells
* Odor   : organic, earthy
* Structure   : stratified, fissured, slick sided
* Cementation   : Medium and coarse sand dominate more than 50%

5.11   Stratified Soils

Term	Thickness
Parting	0-1/16" Seam
	1-16" - 1/2"
Layer	1/2" - 12"
Stratum	> 12"
Varved clay	Alternating seam or layer of sand, silt and clay
Pocket	Small, erratic deposit
Lens	Lenticular deposit
Occasional	Maximum one per 30 cm thickness

Example: Greyish-brown, dry, dense, fine to medium sand with a trace of silt and shell fragments, weakly cemented in parts.

6. FIELD RECORDS

Prepare a separate log for each borehole and preserve it in good condition. The information shall include the following:

6.1   General

- Bore hole number
- Location
- Type of bore hole
- Depth of bore hole
- Ground elevation
- Make and manufacturer of drilling equipment
- Size and type of bit
- Penetration depth and dated and timed rate
- Size and length of casing
- Depth to which casing is driven
- Height of drop and weight of drop hammer for advancement of casing

6.2   Standard Penetration Test

This is to include the number of blows for each of three 15 cm penetration intervals or the number of blows until sampler rejection.

6.3   Soil Sampling

- Number
- Depth interval
- Type
- Hydraulic pressure to push

- Rate of pushing
- Height of drop
- Weight of drop hammer
- Blow count data for each 75 mm penetration or part of it
- Length of drive
- Length of recovery
- Description of soil and thickness of strata

6.4 *Core Sampling*

- Sampler
- Length of core run
- Time of run
- Drill pressure
- Core pressure
- Core recovery
- Rock quality designation (RQD)
- Record of changes in rate of advancement of bit charges

6.5 *Drilling Mud*

- Mud properties, viscosity
- Depth first and last used
- Depth of loss
- Depth of regain

6.6 *Drilling Water*

(Where applicable) * Depth of water lost
* Depth of water regained
* Amount and color of return water

6.7   Depth of Bedrock

- Thickness of overburden
- Thickness of weathered rock
- Depth to bedrock

6.8   Abandoned Boreholes

- Reason for abandoning the boring

6.9   Miscellaneous

- Depth of obstacles encountered, e.g., boulder, squeezing ground or caving material
- Unusual condition, if any, encountered during advancement of boring and sampling, e.g., accident.
- Excavation, use of hand auger
- Addition of water during hand auguring
- Standing time, give reasons
- In-situ test
- Instrumentation
- Grouting

7. PREPARATION OF THE GEOTECHNICAL LOG

A blank drilling log form is provided in Fig. 7, and standard symbols to be used for designating the lithology are given in Fig. 8. The drilling log will be filled as follows:

7.1   Field Record

i.   Depth Record
ii.   Drilling Progress (m):
      1.10.84 - 8.00 hrs.
      Date and time indicating the depth of drilling/
      Sampling / field testing.
iii. Casing Depth (m)
      Casing was advanced 5.0 m below ground level
iv.   Field Testing/Instrumentation
      Piezometer with tip at depth shown. Permeability test was conducted at this depth. Highest recorded water level.
      Lowest recorded water level.
      Water sample taken at this depth.

7.2   Sample Record

i.   Depth - this is to specify the depth at which a sample is obtained.
ii.   Number - this is to identify the sample number.
iii. Sampler
      Key Sampler type:
      R: Ring-lined (ID 63.5 mm) U: Thin wall (ID 73 mm)
      D: Denison double tube (60 mm) S: Split spoon (35 mm)
      G: Drill cutting
      P: Pitcher (73 mm).

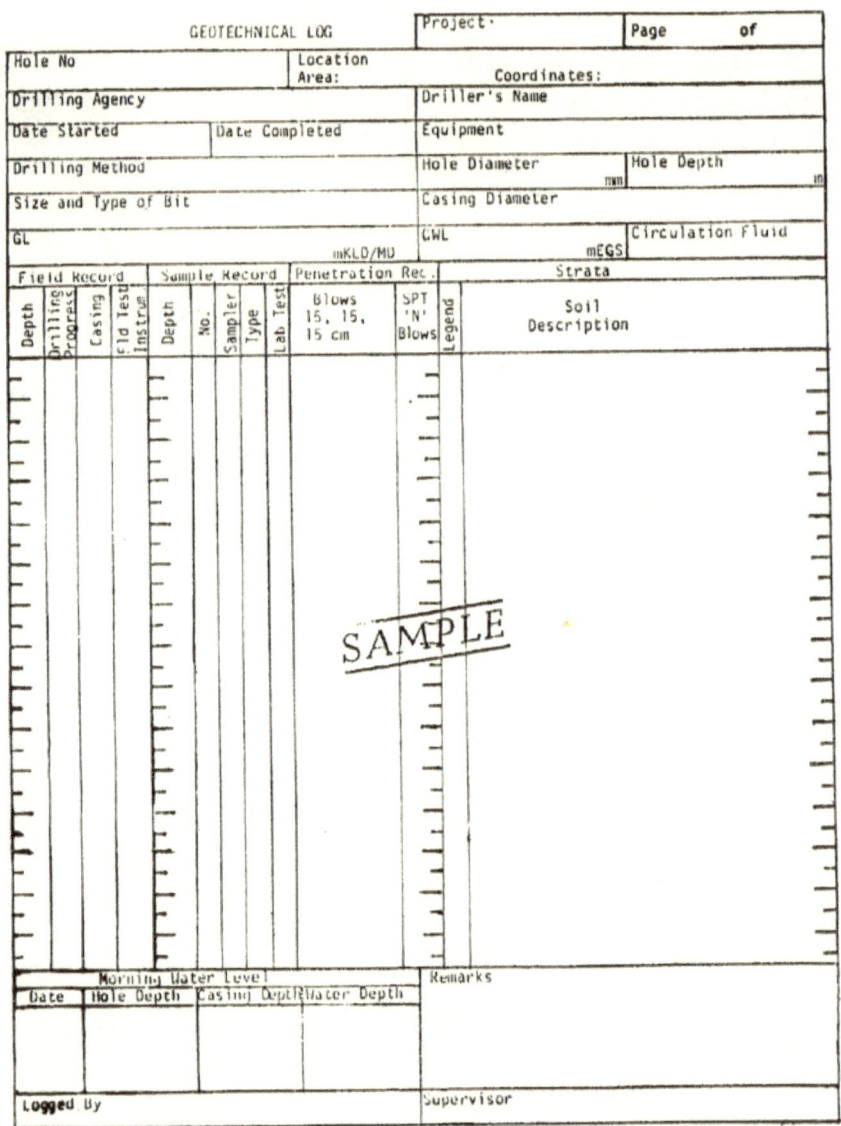

Figure 7. Blank drilling log form.

GEOTECHNICAL LOG		Project WATER RISE IN KUWAIT	Page 1 of 1

Hole No 'KIS/000001	Location Area: Andalus	Coordinates: E 787517.17 N 3251476.55

Drilling Agency GII	Driller's Name Mohammad

Date Started 1.10.84	Date Completed 2.10.8	Equipment Acker-Skid mounted

Drilling Method Rotary	Hole Diameter 101 mm	Hole Depth 9.5 m

Size and Type of Bit 4" Darg	Casing Diameter (mm): 98

GL + 8.25 mKLD/MD	GWL 1.98 mEGS	Circulation Fluid Water

Field Record				Sample Record				Penetration Rec.		Strata	
Depth	Drilling Progress	Casing	Fld Test/Instrum	Depth	No.	Sampler	Type	Lab Test	Blows 15, 15, 15 cm	SPT 'N' Blows	Legend	Soil Description

Blows data / soil description (as read):

- 3,7,10 (40/45) — SPT N = 17 — Pale brown silty fine to medium sand with a trace of coarse sand, a few plant roots.
- Push wait (70/76) — Pale grey medium dense, moist, fine to coarse grained sand, traces of silt and Gravel occasionally weakly cemented. — Do —
- 16,20,20/12 (38/42) — 40/27 — — Do —
- 15,30,45 (35/45) — — Do —
- Push kPa 1400 kPa 100 RPM (35/45) — — Do — End of Boring

Morning Water Level				Remarks
Date	Hole Depth	Casing Depth	Water Depth	1. Light shower on 1.10.84 (10.00–10.30 Hrs), followed by bright sunshine remaining throughout.
1.10.84	2.5	2.0	1.98	2. 12-30-1430: Work delayed due to mechanical trouble with engine.
2.10.84	5.5	5.0	2.00	3. Falling Head Permeability test conducted at 9.00–9.76 m. with casing at 9.00 m.
3.10.84	9.76	—	1.98	4. Stand pipe Piezometer was installed on 2.10.84.

Logged By Ahmad	Supervisor

Figure 8. Completed sample drilling log.

H: Hand auger
iv. Type of Sample
Undisturbed sample
Disturbed sample
Sample attempted, no recovery
v. Laboratory test–x indicates laboratory test to be conducted on the soil sample

7.3 *Penetration Record*

- Disturbed Sampling
  Blows/15, 15, 15 cm: 3, 7, 10 (40/45)
  The number of blows by a 63.5 kg hammer is falling from a height of 76 cm taken to advance the split-spoon sampler through three consecutive 15 cm penetrations. Sample recovery 40 cm out of 45 cm attempted.
  'N' Value: 17 is the chosen value of the succession. 17 blows of the hammer drove the sampler 30 cm after 15 cm seating drive. **Note:** When full penetration has not been achieved, the number of blows for the quoted penetration is given, for example: 20/12 20 blows of the hammer drove sampler a distance of 12 cm
- Undisturbed Sampling
  Blows/15, 15, 15 cm: 15, 30, 45 (35/45)
  The number of blows by a 63.5 kg hammer is falling from a height of 76 cm taken to advance the sampler through three consecutive 15 cm penetrations. Sample recovery 35 cm out of 45 cm attempted.
  Blows/15, 15, 15 cm * 15, 30, 45 (35)
  If driving energy is different, this should be included in REMARKS of the logging sheet
  * Push
    WHO Sampler pushed by the weight of SPT hammer
    (35/45) Sample recovery

* Push

1400

(35/45) This indicates recovery of sample for sampler pushed by a pressure of 1400 kPa

1. Strata
   a. Legends and symbols are as shown in Fig. 9.
   b. Soil description
2. The full water level information to be recorded as directed below.

Recordings were taken at the start of each day's work, except the first one which first struck level.

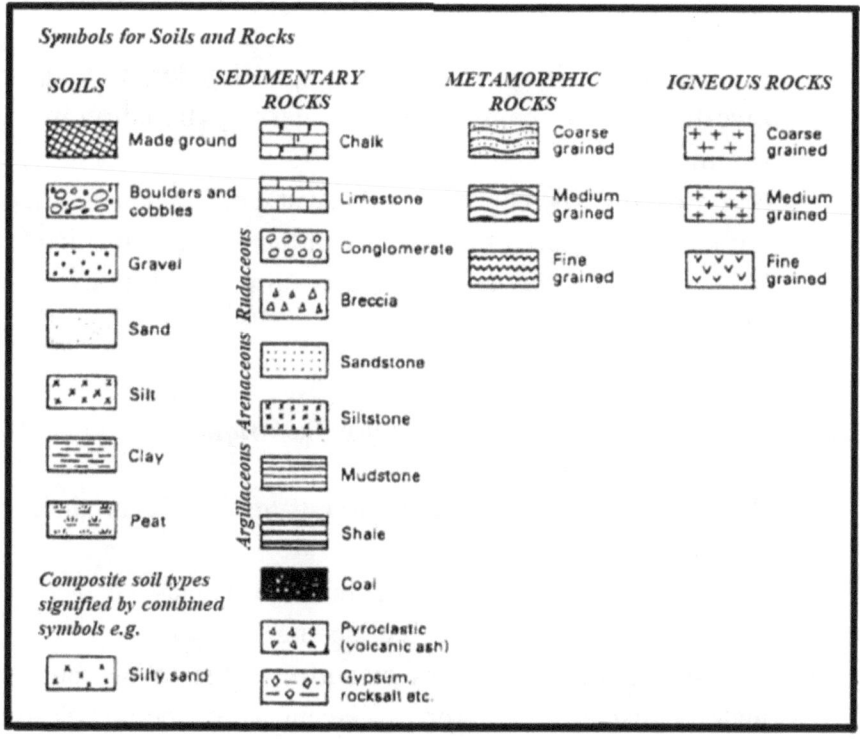

Figure 9. Symbols for soil and rock.

8. FIELD STAFF CHECKLIST

8.1   General

When going to the site, take necessary forms, pencil, paper, a hard board, technical specifications, field manual, field clothes, hard helmet, and safety shoes.

- Discuss any problems encountered by the driller and give a quick decision. Consult technical specifications in case of controversy.
- Deliver all samples to the office at frequent intervals.
- Submit a copy of the drilling record to the office after the day's work.
- Maintain close liaison with the Project Leader, so that the investigation can be modified if necessary, based on initial findings.
- Stop working when light is insufficient. Follow general safety regulations. In case of accident, call the office immediately.
- Instructions for the next day's program should be outlined in advance.

8.2   Drilling/Sampling/Field Testing Technique

- Watch the technique(s) closely to ensure that disturbance of soil is minimized.
- Check that the alignment of the hole is vertical.
- Note if the sides of hole are collapsing.
- Assess the amount of loss of cuttings due to overburden material displacement. Appropriate measures should be taken in the drilling process.

8.3   Depth

- Check the depth of casings to ensure that they never penetrate beneath the bottom of the borehole.
- Check the depth of sampling and field testing to ensure that all sampling and testing are done at the proper depth.

8.4   SPT Soundings

- Check for blocking of vents in sampler head.
- Check out probable sources of error given in section 2.7.
- Check that split spoon sampler is opened at both ends for extraction of soil sample.

8.5   Sampler

- Check for damaged cutting shoes and rusty or dirty sampler.
- Check for jamming of inner barrel in double tube core barrels.

8.6   Sample Storage and Transportation

- Check adequacy of sample sealing and ensure proper labeling.
- Ensure storage of sample at site, so that no moisture will be lost.
- During transportation to the office, handle samples carefully for the least disturbance.

8.7   Drilling Record

- Record every event taking place in the field.
- Describe samples as outlined in Section 5.3.
- Prepare drilling log as outlined in Chapter 7 and Fig. 8.

9. STANDPIPE PIEZOMETER

The simplest form of pore pressure measuring device is the standpipe piezometer. A standpipe piezometer consists of a piezometer tip containing porous element inserted in a borehole and connected via small diameter pipes to the ground level. Many commercial type piezometers (e.g. Cassagrande) are used in Western countries but in Kuwait, the general practice is to perforate the pipe at its lower end to act as the porous tip. The pipe usually made up of PVC material, is 38 to 50mm (ID) and of variable length. The following sizes of pipes and number of perforations are often adopted.

Size of perforation	No. for 38mm Dia. pipe	No. for 50mm Dia. pipe
10 mm dia. holes	30 per meter	50 per meter

The space between the tube perforations and the wall of the bore hole is normally packed with sand or fine gravel, and the top of the hole is then sealed with Bentonite or concrete to prevent the ingress of surface water.

The piezometer is used to determine the hydrostatic pressure at a point in the soil profile. Piezometer pressure at the tip of the perforated/porous body is indicated by the head of water which develops inside the standpipe tubing. This water level is generally measured by lowering a dip meter probe from the ground level.

In WH-001 project, two type of piezometers shall be used. Typical details shown in Fig. 10.

- Shallow piezometer (Up to 10 m)
- Deep piezometer (Deeper than 10 m)

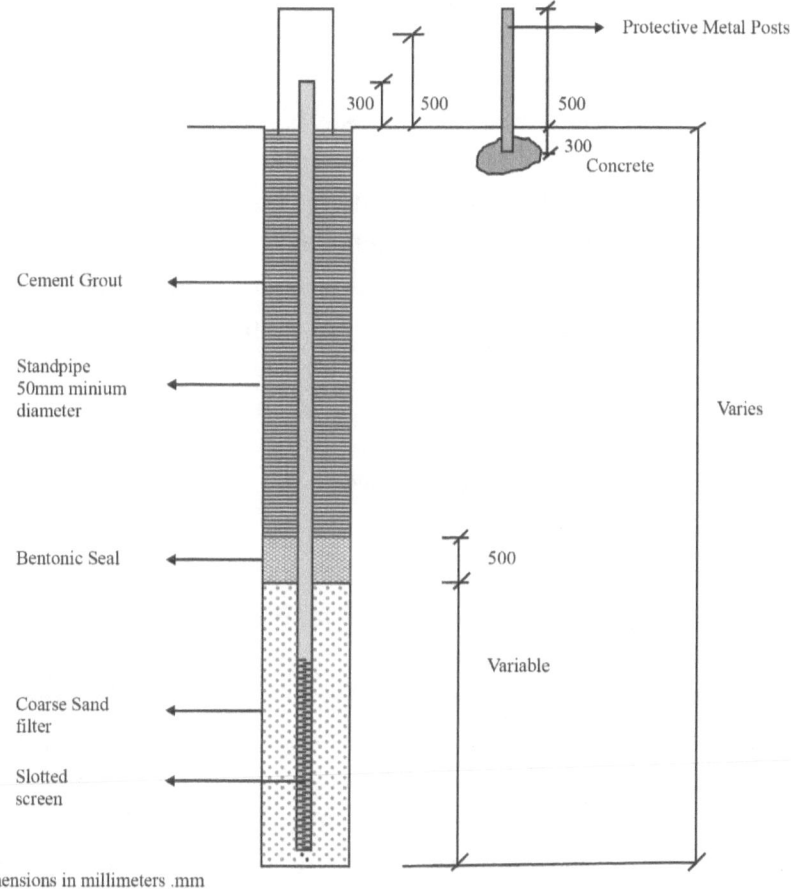

Figure 10. Typical construction of piezometers

9.1   Equipment

- Drill rig
- PVC standpipe (perforated and imperforated)
- Dip meter
- Solvent cement
- Couplings
- End cap
- Metal posts

9.2   *Installation Procedure*

1. Drill hole to specified depth using casing and water as needed (Note: A Bentonite slurry shall NOT be used in drilling).
2. Flush the hole with clean water until all the soil cuttings etc. are removed so that the flushed material is clean water.
3. Check piezometer tube joints against leakage.
4. Wrap the perforated length 2 mm nylon mesh. Flush clean water through the system before the piezometer is lowered into the borehole.
5. Place the perforated tip at least 50 cm above the bottom of the borehole. Pour clean and well-rounded sand (No. 20 to No. 10 US sieve mesh) to fill the annular space around the perforated pipe.
6. Start with drawing casing (if used) gradually in such a way that the bottom of casing remains at least one meter below the top of backfill.
7. Use a 0.5 m thick cement Bentonite grout seal on top of sand backfill. The proportion shall be Bentonite: Cement: Water = 1:20:20.
8. Backfill the rest of the borehole with approved grout.
9. Use protective metal casing from 0.5 m below the ground surface to extend above the top of piezometer. Grout the surroundings to prevent rain water entering the ground around the piezometer pipe.
10. Flush the pipe on routine basis particularly when it is clogged.
11. Take reading of water level in the piezometer pipe on daily basis for the first week after its installation and then, at least, twice a week.
12. Seal the piezometer pipe with suitable cap.
13. Place brightly painted frame or fence around the piezometer so that it can be seen from a distance.
14. Maintain a log of piezometer installation (Fig. 11).
15. Take the elevation of the top of the piezometer pipe.

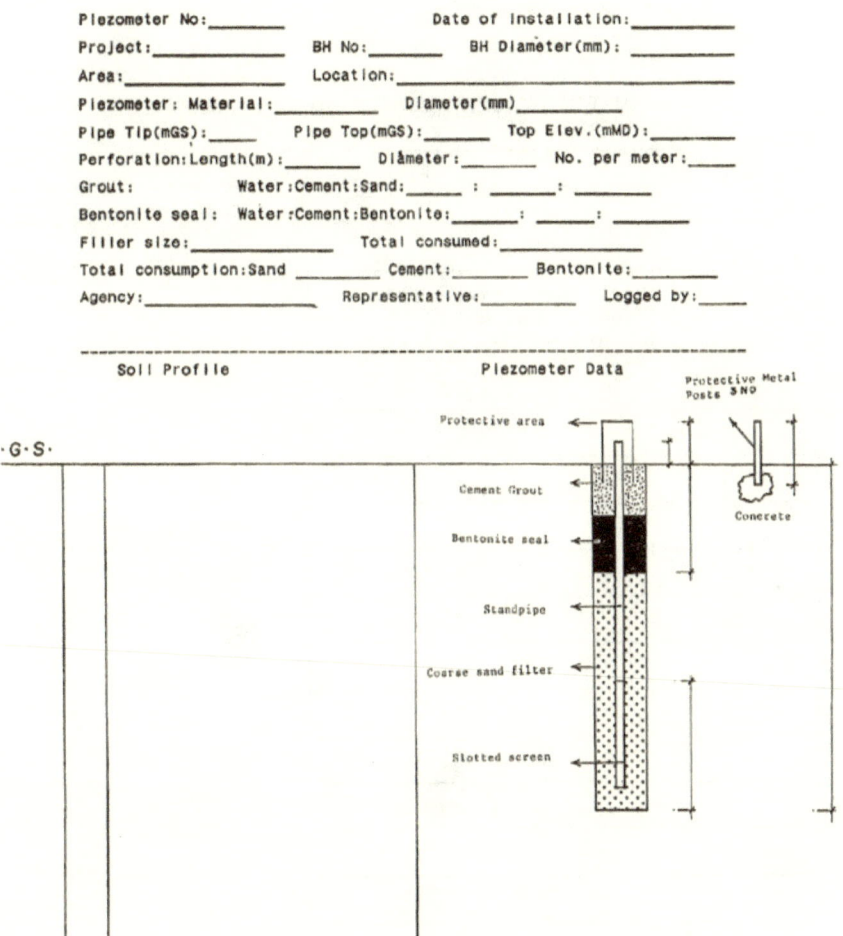

Figure 11. Piezometer installation log

9.3   Groundwater monitoring

A groundwater monitoring data sheet is given in Fig. 12.

GROUNDWATER MONITORING DATA SHEET

Project :_____

Piezometer No:_____   Piez.top (m MD):_____   GL:_____

BH :_____ __   Area:_____   Coordinates:_____

Date .	Time	Depth to GWL from Piez.top (m)	Elev. of GW (m)	Logged by

Figure 12. Groundwater monitoring data sheet.

10. IN-SITU PERMEABILITY TEST

The principle of this method is to drill a hole to the required depth. When water comes to equilibrium, some water is poured in or bailed out. The rate at which water seeps back into the hole is measured and using a suitable formula, the coefficient of permeability (k) can be computed *(US Department of Navy, 1982)* according to (Fig. 13). The field determination of 'k' has a shortcoming that it is largely dependent on how best the soil geometry and other parameters are ascertained in the field. Shape Factors (S) mentioned in Fig. 13a&b, are obtainable from Figure14

In the following sections, the formula to be used in computations, is based on the assumptions of an infinite and isotropic soil. The reliability of values obtainable are, therefore, dependent on the homogeneity of the stratum and on certain restrictions of the mathematical formula used.

10.1. *Variable Head method*

This test can be conducted in bore holes lined with casing *(US Department of Navy, 1982)*, (Figs. 15 & 16) as well as in Piezometers (Fig. 17). This test is also suitable for conducting at various depths during the progress of the boring provided the test section will stand unsupported. The whole test section must be below the ground water level. The test can be conducted using the Falling Head method, as well as Rising Head Method.

10.1.1 *Falling Head method*

Equipment:

• Drill rig

- Water level indicator
- Stop watch
- Casing or Piezometer (whichever applicable)

CONDITION	DIAGRAM	SHAPE FACTOR F	PERMEABILITY, K BY VARIABLE HEAD TEST	APPLICABILITY
			FOR OBSERVATION WELL OF CONSTANT CROSS SECTION	
(A) UNCASED HOLE	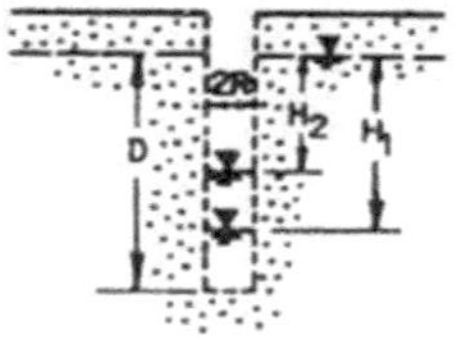	$F = 16 \pi DSR$	$K = \dfrac{R}{16DS} \times \dfrac{(H_2 - H_1)}{(t_2 - t_1)}$ FOR $\dfrac{D}{R} < 50$	Simplest method for permeability determination not applicable in stratified soils. For values of S, see Figure 14.
(B) CASED HOLE, SOIL FLUSH WITH BOTTOM.	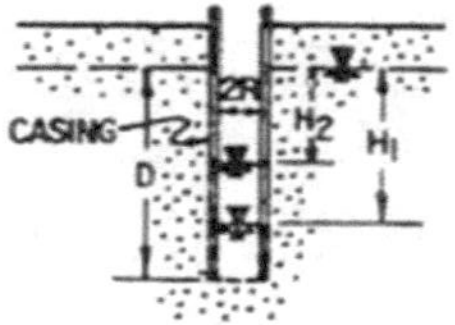	$F = \dfrac{11R}{2}$	$K = \dfrac{2\pi R}{11(t_2 - t_1)} \ln\left(\dfrac{H_1}{H_2}\right)$ FOR $6'' \leq D \leq 60''$	Used for permeability determination at shallow depths below water table, may yield unreliable results in falling head test with silting of bottom of hole.

Note: Observation well or piezometer in saturated isotropic stratum of infinite depth

Figure 13a. Variable head test in observation well

CONDITION	DIAGRAM	SHAPE FACTOR F	PERMEABILITY, K BY VARIABLE HEAD TEST	APPLICABILITY
(C) CASED HOLE, UNCASED OR PERFORATED EXTENSION OF LENGTH "L".	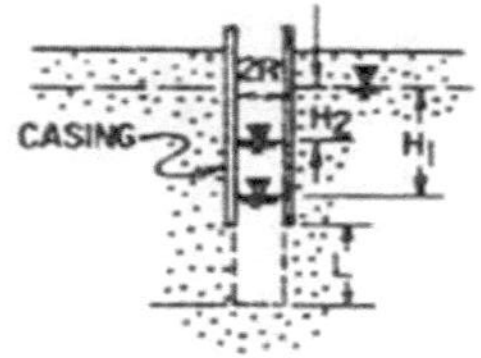	$F = \dfrac{2\pi L}{\ln\left(\dfrac{L}{R}\right)}$	$K = \dfrac{R^2}{2L(t_2-t_1)}\ln\left(\dfrac{L}{R}\right)\ln\left(\dfrac{H_1}{H_2}\right)$ FOR $\dfrac{L}{R} > 8$	*Used for permeability determination at greater depths below water table.*
(D) CASED HOLE, COLUMN OF SOIL INSIDE CASING TO HEIGHT "L".	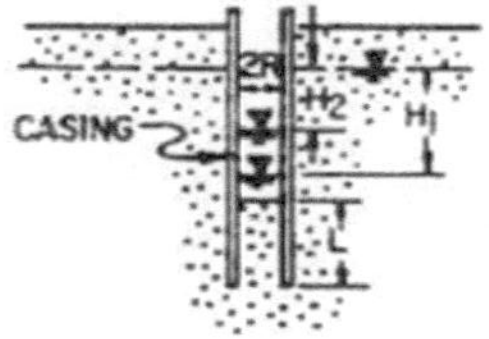	$F = \dfrac{11\pi R^2}{2\pi R + 11 L}$	$K = \dfrac{2\pi R + 11 L}{11(t_2-t_1)}\ln\left(\dfrac{H_1}{H_2}\right)$	*Principal use is for permeability in vertical direction in anisotropic soils*

Note: Observation well or piezometer in saturated isotropic stratum of infinite dept

Figure 13b. Variable head test in observation well

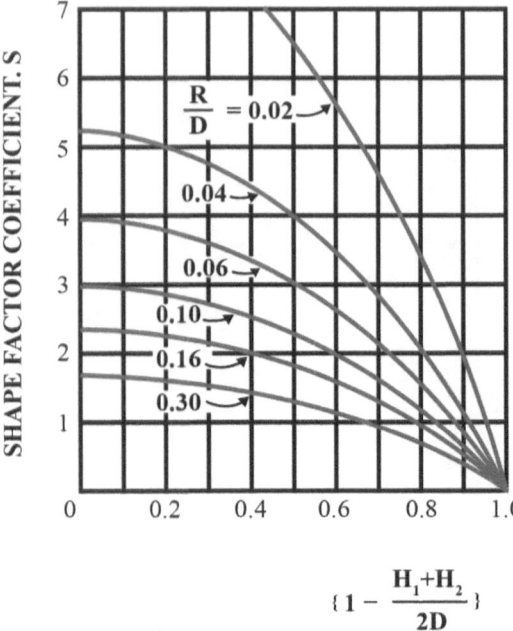

$$\{ 1 - \frac{H_1 + H_2}{2D} \}$$

Figure 14. Shape factor coefficient

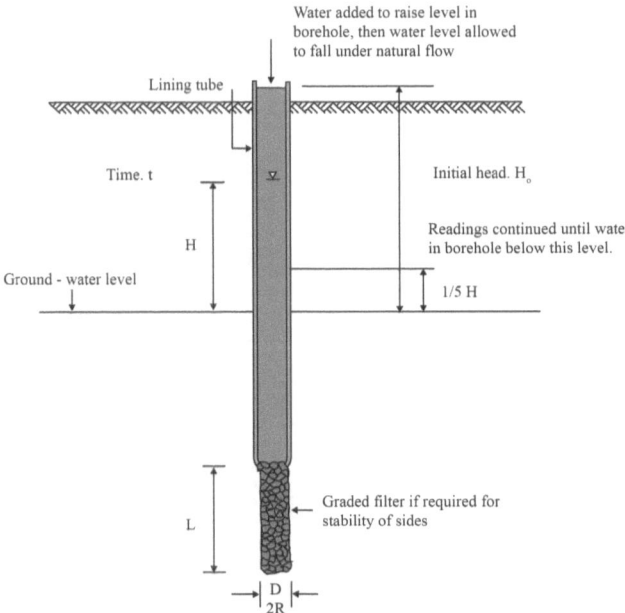

Figure 15. Falling head test

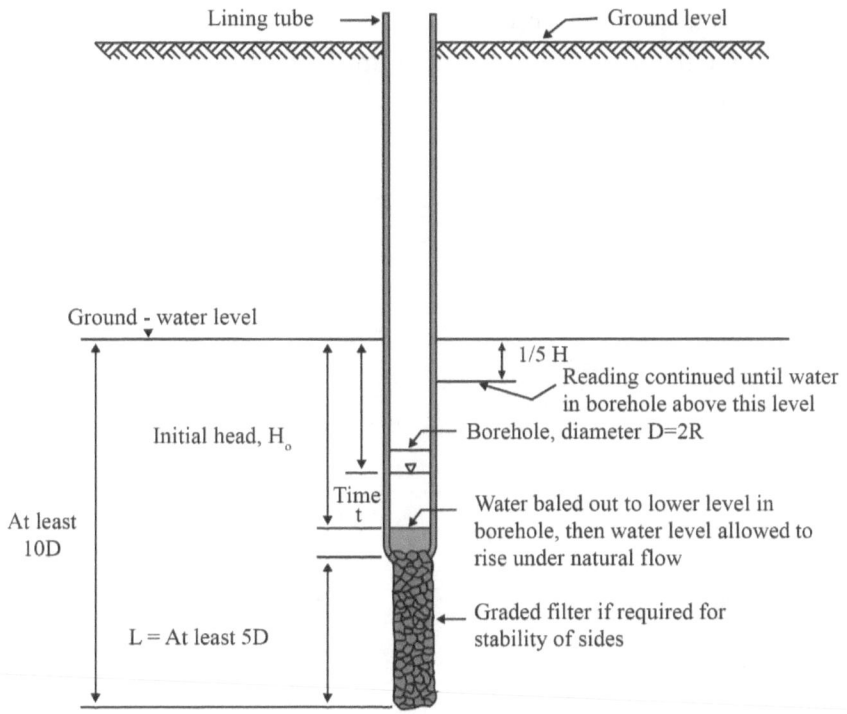

Figure 16. Rising head test.

Procedure

1. Advance the borehole to the depth of test using suitable method. Clean the hole by flushing sufficient water until it is clear of all debris and the flushed liquid is clean water. Wait until water level reaches equilibrium state (level of water inside and outside borehole same).

2. In case of cased hole with uncased or perforated extension, casing must be taken down initially to the full depth. Place suitable sand fill in the borehole while withdrawing the casing to expose the required length of the unlined hole for the test. The sand fill should be just above the bottom of the casing.

3. Record the equilibrium water level in the hole.
4. Add clean water to the borehole to raise the water level as high as possible (preferably to top of hole).
5. Keep the water level constant until all air bubbles are allowed to escape.

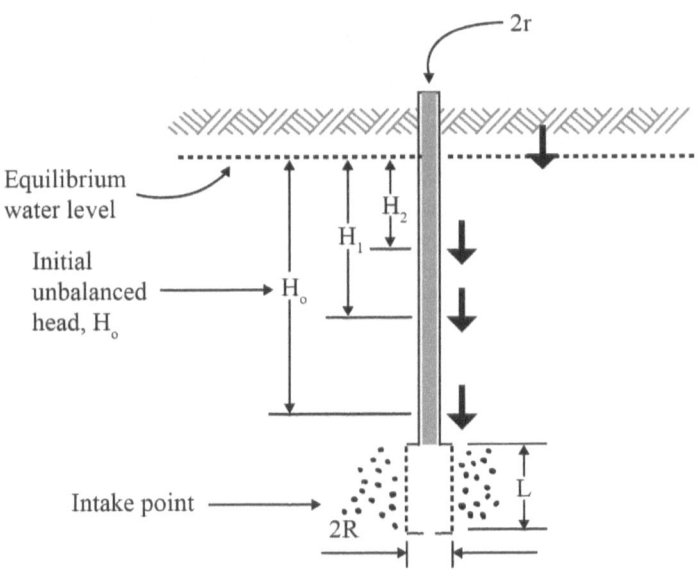

Radius of intake point (R) differes from radius of standpipe (r) :

$$F = \frac{2\pi L}{\ln\left(\frac{L}{R}\right)}$$

$$A = \pi r^2$$

$$K = \frac{A}{F\,(t_2 - t_1)} \ln\left(\frac{H_1}{H_2}\right)$$

$$K = \frac{r^2}{2L} \ln\left(\frac{L}{R}\right) \left[\frac{\ln(H_1/H_2)}{(t_2 - t_1)}\right]$$

Figure 17. Variable head test in piezometer.

6. Remove the source water. No more water shall be added during the test.

7. Take reading of the water level at frequent time intervals, each time reading both the elapsed time and water level.

The frequency of readings will depend on the rate of fall of the water level. As a guide reading should be taken such that each level differs from the previous reading by about the same height as follows:-

>   Head of water in borehole above GL > 2m: reading interval 5 - 10 cm
>   Head of water in borehole above GL < 2m: reading interval 1 to 2 cm

8. In case of standpipe piezometers, install the piezometer as detailed in section
   Repeat steps 3 through 8.

9. Record the following data
   - Diameter of unlined borehole at test section and diameter of casing.
   - Depth of BH below G.L.
   - Depth of casing.
   - Height of datum above G.L.
   - Depth to equilibrium GWL below datum or GL.
   - Instant GWL and corresponding elapsed time.

10.1.2 Rising Head method

This test can be conducted in cased holes as well as in piezometers provided bailing or pumping out of water is practicable. The bore hole must penetrate below groundwater level by at least 10 times its diameter (ID).

Equipment

- Drill rig
- Water pump
- Water level indicator
- Stop watch
- Casing

Procedure

1. Prepare borehole and test section in the same way as detailed in Falling Head method.
2. Record the equilibrium water level in the bore hole.
3. Bail out water to just above the bottom end of casing.
4. Immediately after bailing, start taking readings of water level at various time intervals. Continue recording until the difference between the water level in the borehole and groundwater level is not more than 1/5th of the initial difference in these levels.
5. Record the data listed in step 9 of Falling Head method.

   A blank data recording sheet is given in Fig. 18. And for more details see Fig 18a.

10.1.3 Data Reduction

The coefficient of permeability is calculated using the equations given by U.S. Department of Navy, 1982 in (Fig. 13).

These formulae are based on the assumptions of an infinite and isotropic soil.

10.2 Double Packer method

The Packer test also known as Lugeon test (Lugeon, 1933). The double packer test as shown in Fig. 19 can be carried at a variety of depths using a double packer to seal the test section top and bottom. This test is used to determine the value of the horizontal coefficient of permeability for that particular section.

Equipment

- Drill rig
- Packers
- Stop watch
- Water swivel

FIELD PERMEABILITY TEST
(Falling / Rising Head method)

Project	: _____	Agency	: _____	Date	: _____
BH No.	: _____	Area	: _____	Location	: _____
RL. of casing top	: _____	Ht . of casing top	: _____	Depth of GWL	: _____
BH Depth	: _____	Casing depth	: _____	Soil	: _____
H_O	: _____	BH Dia. (2R)	: _____	Piezo dia. (2r)	: _____
Contractor's rep	: _____			logged by	: _____

Figure 18. Field permeability test (data sheet).

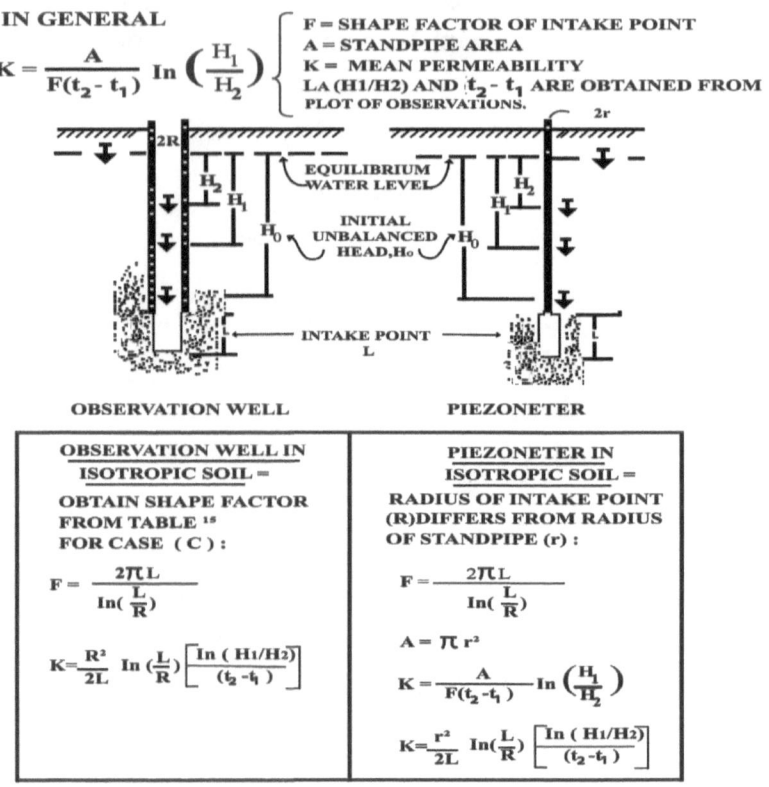

IN GENERAL

$$K = \frac{A}{F(t_2 - t_1)} \ln\left(\frac{H_1}{H_2}\right)$$

F = SHAPE FACTOR OF INTAKE POINT
A = STANDPIPE AREA
K = MEAN PERMEABILITY
LA (H1/H2) AND $t_2 - t_1$ ARE OBTAINED FROM
PLOT OF OBSERVATIONS.

OBSERVATION WELL   PIEZONETER

OBSERVATION WELL IN ISOTROPIC SOIL =	PIEZONETER IN ISOTROPIC SOIL =
OBTAIN SHAPE FACTOR FROM TABLE [15] FOR CASE (C):	RADIUS OF INTAKE POINT (R)DIFFERS FROM RADIUS OF STANDPIPE (r) :
$F = \dfrac{2\pi L}{\ln\left(\frac{L}{R}\right)}$	$F = \dfrac{2\pi L}{\ln\left(\frac{L}{R}\right)}$
$K = \dfrac{R^2}{2L} \ln\left(\frac{L}{R}\right)\left[\dfrac{\ln(H_1/H_2)}{(t_2 - t_1)}\right]$	$A = \pi r^2$
	$K = \dfrac{A}{F(t_2 - t_1)} \ln\left(\frac{H_1}{H_2}\right)$
	$K = \dfrac{r^2}{2L} \ln\left(\frac{L}{R}\right)\left[\dfrac{\ln(H_1/H_2)}{(t_2 - t_1)}\right]$

Figure 18a. Field permeability test (data sheet).

Procedure

1. Advance the hole to the depth of test using suitable method, surge it and bail it out.
2. Set two packers on perforated pipe or drill rod and inflate them using gas pressure supplied from a nitrogen bottle. The length of packers when expanded should be at least 5D where D is the diameter of the hole. (The longer the packers used, the more effective will be the test). The test section is often about 3 m long.
3. Plug the bottom of the pipe holding the pack.
4. Bail out water at the constant rate through the drill rod. Record the quantity bailed out.

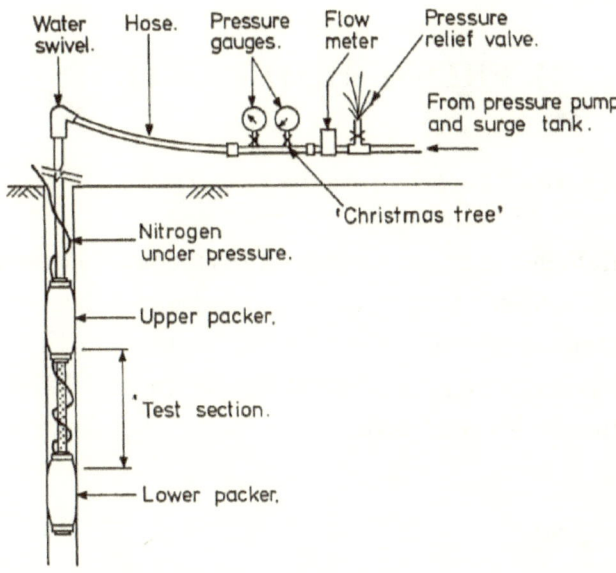

Figure 19. Double Packer test for soil permeability

10.2.1 Data reduction

The co-efficient of permeability is calculated using the formula (Earth Manual, 1974).

Table 1. Values of Cp. (After Earth Manual, 1974

Length of test section in feet, L	C_p values			
	Diameter of test hole			
	EX	AX	BX	NX
1	31,000	28,500	25,800	23,300
2	19,400	18,100	16,800	15,500
3	14,400	13,600	12,700	11,800
4	11,600	11,000	10,300	9,700
5	9,800	9,300	8,800	8,200
6	8,500	8,100	7,600	7,200
7	7,500	7,200	6,800	6,400
8	6,800	6,500	6,100	5,800
9	6,200	5,900	5,600	5,300
10	5,700	5,400	5,200	4,900
15	4,100	3,900	3,700	3,600
20	3,200	3,100	3,000	2,800

11. PRESSUREMETER TESTS

11.1   Purpose of Test

Pressuremeter tests are field tests performed to give profiles of shear modulus, in-situ horizontal stress, undrained shear strength, and co-efficient of horizontal consolidation. The test was first introduced some 30 years ago by Lois Menard (Baguelin et al 1978) and it has been practiced with considerable success all over the world.

11.2   The probe

Pressuremeters (Fig. 20) are broadly defined as cylindrical devices designed to apply uniform pressures to the walls of a borehole

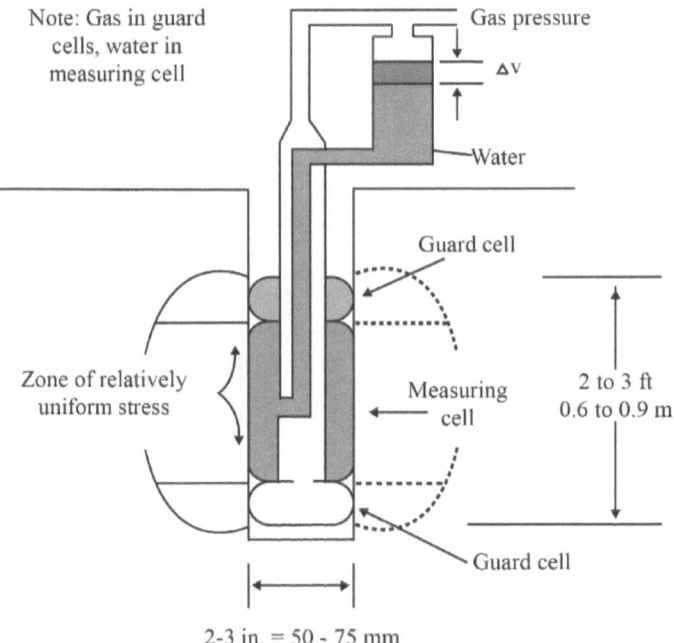

Figure 20. Menard pressuremeter

by means of a flexible membrane. The membranes are expanded against the surrounding soils by means of water, gas or oil under pressure causing outward radial expansion of the soil.

11.3 Self Boring Pressuremeter (SBP)

The SBP is a hollow cylindrical probe shown in Fig.21 *(Wetland and Head, 1983)* about 1m in length and 80mm in diameter. The instrument has a composite membrane made from urethane protected by a sheath of flexible stainless steel strips bonded to a rubber sleeve. The radial expansion of the membrane is monitored at 3 places using transducers.

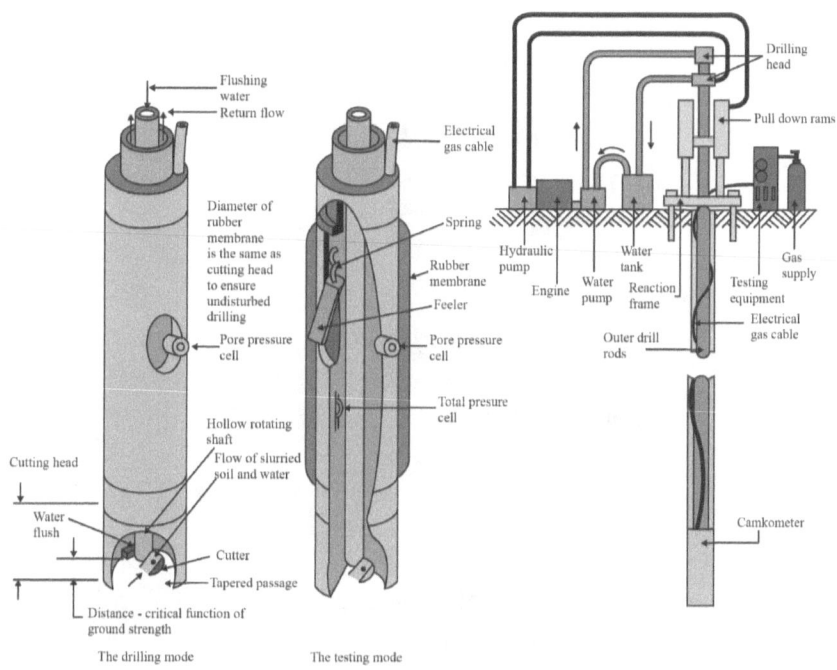

Figure 21. Self-boring pressuremeter.

This probe, operated from a purpose built rig, bores its way into the ground. It can be used in most soil including weak rocks and hence considered suitable for Kuwaiti cemented soils.

- Special built rig consists of:
    - Engine
    - Hydraulic pump
    - Water pump
    - Water Tank

  The various units with principal accessories are

- Probe
    - Hollow metal tube
    - Stainless steel tubes and fittings
    - Rubber cell membrane
    - Sheath
    - O-rings

- Control unit
    - Volumeter and its graduated scale
    - Pressure gauges
    - Umbilicus

- Circuit unit
    - Semi-rigid polyamide co-axial tubing

- Oil or gas supply

11.4   Calibration

It is important to carry out calibrations (Appendix 'A') to determine the compliance of the testing equipment and measuring devices.

11.5   Procedure

1. Bore and clean the hole satisfactorily
2. Install the probe at the depth of test

3. De-air the system completely
4. Raise pressure in a series of equal increments (10-12 increments). The increments are 50 kPa for stiff soil and 100 kPa for weak rock or cemented soil.
5. Maintain each pressure increment for 2 minutes. Take readings of change of volume (Figure 22) at 15, 30, 60 and 120 seconds. A typical calibration curve is given in Fig. 22, **curve obtained with 60 mm rubber membrane probe inside 76 mm slotted steel casing.**

11.6 Data Reduction

• Apply correction (see calibration) to the measurement of pressure, volume as in Appendix 'A' to account for the system compressibility, elevation difference, and rubber membrane characteristics.
• Obtain relationship between corrected pressure and corrected volume of the cavity.

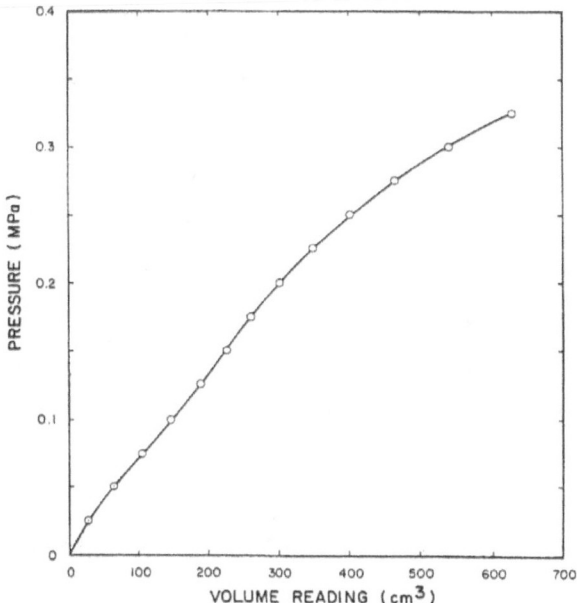

Figure 22. Typical calibration

Blank data sheets and typical plots are given in Figs. 23 - 26.

Pressuremeter Test Data

Project:_____   Agency:_____   Date:_____
BH No : _____   Area:_____   Location:_____
BH Dia:_____   Drill:_____   Soil :_____
Depth: _____   Gauge Ht:_____   W.L.:_____
Volumeter No:_____   Probe Dia:_____   Membrane/
                                                        Sheath :_____

Rec.Press.Diff.:_____   Water Press:_____   Diff.Reqd:_____
Contractor's rep.:_____   Logged by:_____

Pressure (kPa)	Time (sec)	Volume (cc)	Guard cell Press. or Diff. Pr. (kPa)	Creep (cc) (V60-30)	Change (cc) (V60-60)

Remarks:-

Figure 23. Pressuremeter test data.

Pressuremeter Test Data Reduction

Project:_____   Agency:_____   Date:_____

BH No : _____   Area:_____   Location:_____

BH Dia: _____   Type:_____   Soil : _____

Depth : _____   Gauge Ht:_____   W.L.: _____

Volumeter No:_____   Probe Dia:_____   Membrane:_____

Water Press:_____   Vo:_____   Sheath:_____

Hydr.Calculated by:_____   Checked by:_____

Pres in volumeter (kPa)	1 min Volumeter reading (cc)	Total Press (kPa)	Volume corrected (cc)	Corrected Volume (cc)	Membrane resis- tance (kPa)	Corrected pressure (kPa)

Remarks:-

Figure 24. Pressuremeter test data reduction.

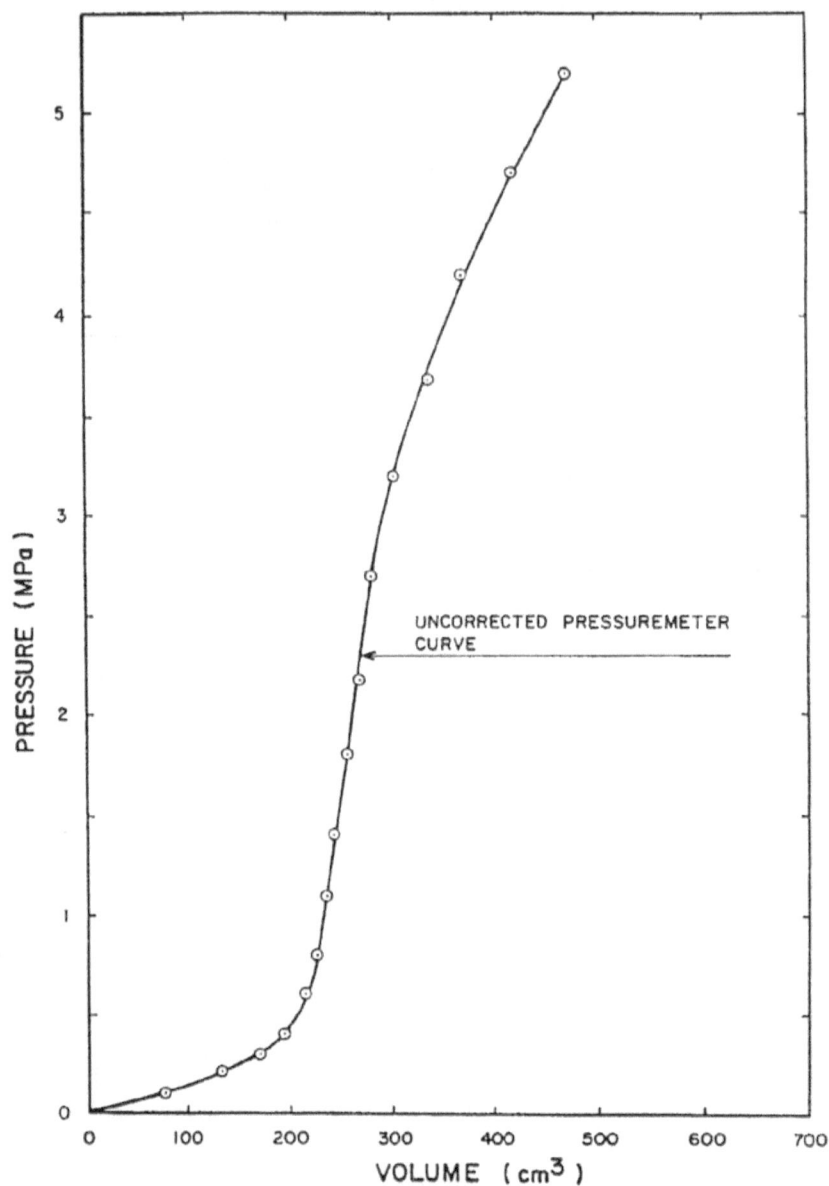

Figure 25. Typical record of a pressuremeter test.

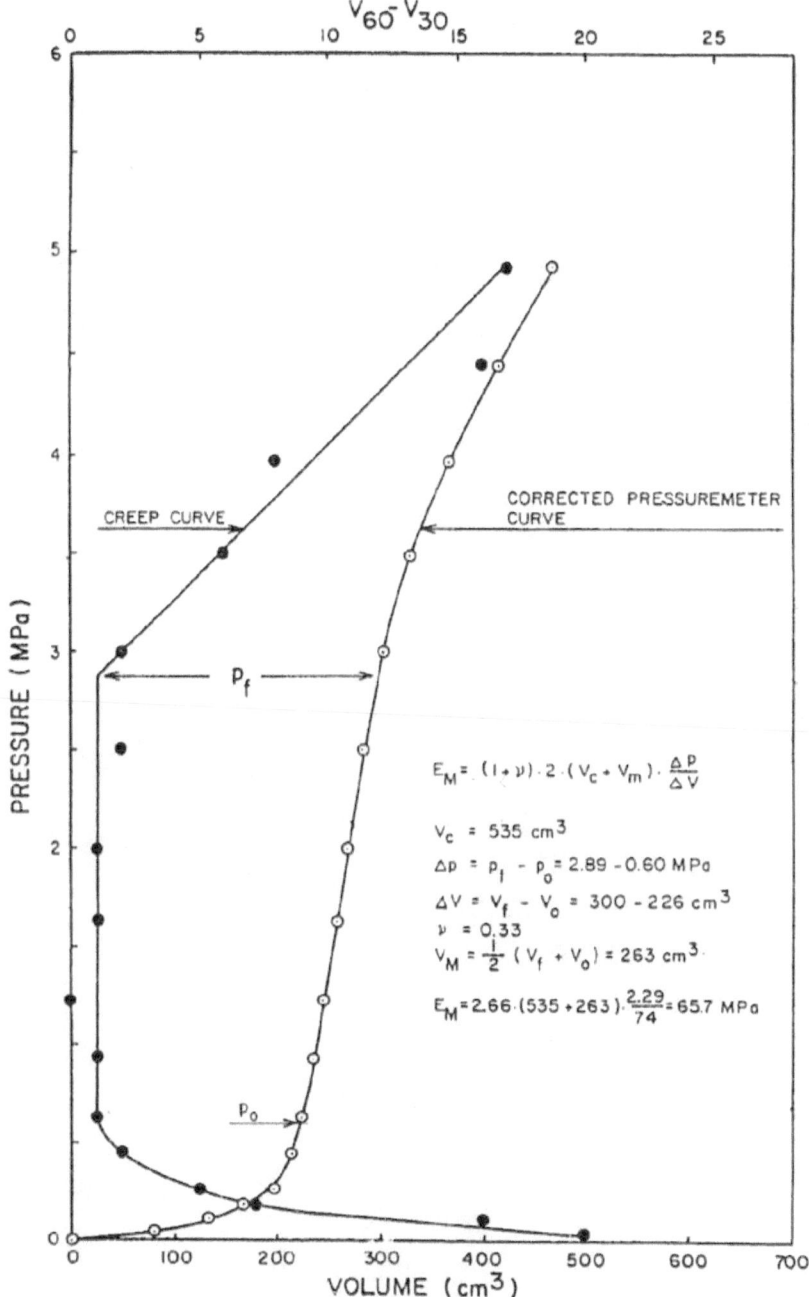

Figure 26. Evaluation of a pressuremeter test record.

APPENDIX 'A'

CALIBRATION OF PRESSUREMETER

1. Calibration of Volume losses

Volume losses are due to
  I.   Line and control unit flexibility (expansion of tubing)
  II. System compliance (compression of rubber membrane and sheath, and compression of water).

1.1. Calibration of Probe, tubing and Steel tube.

1.1.1. Equipment

- Probe unit
- Control unit
- Circuit unit
- Steel tube

1.1.2 Procedure

1. Insert the probe vertically into a close fitting, thick walled and in deformable steel tube.
2. Inflate the probe first to seat against the side of the tube.
3. Apply pressure to the probe in a series of small increments say 100 kPa at the beginning (This inflation will cause seating of the probe against the side of the tube to have a good contact). Increase the pressure to large increments (300 to 400 kPa) until the maximum working pressure is reached. (Since the probe cannot inflate further, any volume change will

be due to the losses in the pressuremeter). Hold each increment for 1 minute taking reading at 15, 30 & 60s.

4. Plot pressure vs. volume reading. Find the point of good contact by drawing tangent to the straight line portion and then extend it back to zero.

1.2 Calibration of Control unit and Tubing without Probe

1.2.1 Equipment:
- Control unit
- Circuit unit

1.2.2 Procedure

1. Block the end of tubing with a special valve fitting designed for the purpose
2. De-air the control unit and tubing
3. Apply pressure in increments of 100 kPa initially and 200 kPa subsequently. Hold each increment for 1 minute. Take readings at interval of 15, 30 and 60s.
4. Plot pressure vs. volume reading. Determine the volume loss between 0 and the good contact pressure. Subtract this volume from the extension to zero (section 1.1.2 step 4). This is the reference for volume calibration (V_r).
5. Calculate volume correction as follows:-

$$\text{Volume correction at Pressure (P)}$$
$$= \text{Volumereading at P} - V_r$$

6. Plot Pressure vs. volume correction data (Fig. A.1)

2. Calibration of Pressure losses

As the probe inflates, a certain amount of pressure is necessary to overcome the resistance of the rubber membrane and the sheath. Thus the pressure which is actually applied to the soil is less than the pressure in the probe.

2.1 Equipment:

- Probe unit
- Control unit
- Circuit unit

2.2 Procedure

1. Place the probe upright on the ground surface
2. Inflate the probe slowly using 10-12 increments of pressure until it is extended to its maximum working volume. (The size of increment can be calculated from the pressure required to work the membrane 4 to 5 times before the calibration is made). Hold the pressure for one minute at each increment. Take volume readings at 15, 30 and 60 seconds.
3. Calculate the actual pressure (Pa) in the probe as follows:-

$$Pa = Pm + rw. ho$$

Where

Pm = the gauge pressure
rw = the unit weight of water
ho = difference in elevation between the gauges of control unit and the middle of measuring cell during the calibration.

4. Plot corrected pressure is volume reading (Fig. A.1). Blank data sheets for recording calibration data are given in Figs. A.2 and A.3.

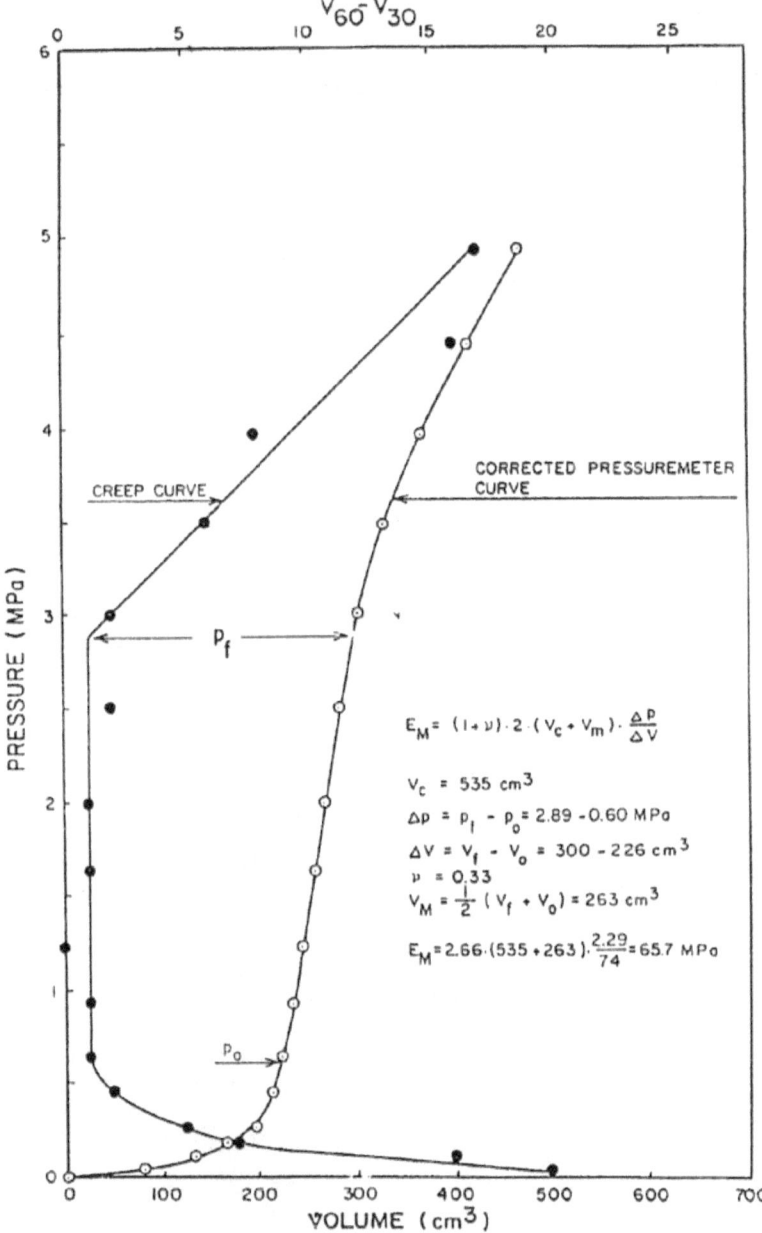

Figure A.1. Evaluation of a pressuremeter test record.

PRESSUREMETER TEST

Volume Calibration

Calibration for: Probe & Tubing inside Steel tube / Control unit & tubing without Probe.

Project   :_____   Agency :_____   Date :_____
Unit   :_____   Membrane:_____   Sheath:_____
Probe Dia:_____   ho =   Recom.Pr.Diff:_____
  Vc   :_____   Contractor's rep:_____   Calib.by:_____

Pressure (kPa)	Diff. Press. (kPa)	Time (sec)	Volume (cc)	Volume correction (cc)

Remarks:-

Figure A-2

149

Pressuremeter Test

CALIBRATION OF MEMBRANE RESISTANCE

Calibration No:_____   Date:_____

Project:_____   Agency:_____

BH No : _____   Area:_____   Location:_____

Unit : _____   Sheath:_____   Membrane:_____

Prob dia:_____   ho : ____ m = ____ kPa

Recom. press. diff:_____Vc:_____

Contractor's rep.:_____   Logged by:_____

Pres.(kPa)	Diff. Press.(kPa)	Time (sec)	Vol (cc)	Corr.P. (kPa)

Press.(kPa)	Diff Press(kPa)	Time (cc)	Vol (cc)	Corr. Press(kPa)

Remarks:-

Figure A-3

BIBLIOGRAPHY

Acker, W. L., III. (1974). Basic procedures for soil sampling and core drilling. Acker Drill Co. Inc., Pa.

ASTM D 1586: (1984). Penetration test and split-barrel sampling of soils. Annual Book of ASTM Standards, Philadelphia. pp.298-303.

ASTM D422-63. (1972) (Reapproved). Standard method for particle size analysis of soils. Annual Book of ASTM Standards, Philadelphia, Pa.

BS5930: 1981. Code of practice for site investigations. British Standards Institution, London. pp.117-118.

Baguelin, F., J.F. Jezquel and D.H. Shields (1978). The Pressuremeter and Foundation Engineering, Trans Tech Publications, Clausthal, West Germany.

Burmister, D.M. (1948). Discussion on soils classification. *Transactions, ASCE* 113:971-977.

Campbell, M. D., and J. H. Lehr. (1973). *Water Well Technology.* New York, McGraw-Hill.

Claton, C.R.I., N. E. Simons, and M. C. Mathews. (1982). *Site Investigation.* London: Granada Publishing.

Dietrich, R. V., J. T. Dutro and R. M. Fosse. (1982). AGI Data Sheets, 2nd, Falls Church, Virginia; American Geological Institute.

Earth Manual (1974), Reprinted (1980), US Department of Interior, Water and Power Resources Service, Washington D.C.

Graton, L.C., and H. J. Fraser. (1935). Systematic packing of spheres - with particular relation to porosity and permeability: Journal of Geology, 43:785-909.

Johnson Division, Universal Oil Products. (1972). *Ground Water and Wells.* Johnson Division, Universal Oil Products Co., Saint Paul, Minnesota 55165.

Joyce, M. D. 1982. Site Investigation Practice. E & F. N. Spon Ltd. Kruseman, G.P., and N. A. De Ridder. (1976). Analysis and evaluating of pumping test data. International Institute for Land Reclamation and Improvement, Bulletin 11, Wageningen, The Netherlands.

Lewis, D.W. (1984). *Practical Sedimentology.* Stroudsburg, Pennsylvania: Hutchinson Ross Publishing Co.

Lugeon, M (1933) Barrages at Geologia, Dunod, Paris.

McKee, E. D., and G. W. Weir. (1953). Terminology for stratification and cross-stratification in sedimentary rocks. *Geological Society of America Bulletin* 64:381-390.

Shephard, F. P., and R. Young. 1961. Distinguishing between beach and dune sands. *Journal of Sedimentary Petrology* 31:196-214.

Teng, W. C. 1962. *Foundation Design.* London: Prentice-Hall.

Terzaghi, K. and Peck, R. B. 1948. *Soil Mechanics in Engineering Practice.* New York: John Wiley and Sons.

U.S. Department of Navy (1982), Soil Mechanics, Design Manual 7.1, Alexandria, Va.

Walton, W. C. 1970. *Ground Water Resource Evaluation.* New York: McGraw-Hill Book Company.

Wintercorn, H. F. and N. Y. Fang. 1975. *Foundation Engineering*

www.ingramcontent.com/pod-product-compliance
Lightning Source LLC
Chambersburg PA
CBHW032026290526
45786CB00011B/509